M000020852

SALTWATER FISHING

Robert Anderson

A Great Outdoors Book

Great Outdoors Publishing Co.
St. Petersburg, Florida

ISBN 0-8200-0128-7

Dedication

To my wife Dorothy, my daughter Robin,
and my sons Craig, Bruce and Rickey.
All have enjoyed the sport of fishing
with an appreciative husband and father.

Printed in the United States of America

Table of Illustrations, continued

Table of Contents, continued

Table of Illustrations

Table of Contents

Table of Contents, continued

Table of Illustrations, continued

Robert Anderson is a man of varied interests, most of them related in one way or another to the great outdoors. He has long had a consuming interest in — and knowledge of — snakes. He is also a devoted bird-watcher. A biologist by education and a motion picture cameraman by trade, he is a Florida outdoorsman by lifestyle. Fishing Florida waters has been high on his list of outdoor activities throughout the thirty years he has lived here.

He has filmed documentaries for all the major TV networks; he served as a director of photography on the *Gentle Ben* and the *Flipper* series and has authored a number of books, most on wildlife and its environment. His *Wilderness Florida* was published earlier this year by VP Publications.

Wearing our Distributor-of-Florida-Books hat, we have in the past sold some of Bob's published books. But we had never met him until he showed up recently, not with a manuscript but with his *Salt Water Fishing* completed and ready for the printer. His hope was that we'd place our colophon on it, a kind of transition from the great outdoors to the Great Outdoors. We were happy to comply and to add it to our list of fishing titles. Herewith is Bob's manual for landing the ones that got away — from boat, surf or pier. Happy angling!

The Publishers

ACKNOWLEDGEMENTS

The author wishes to express his thanks to the National Marine Fisheries Service, an agency of NOAA (the National Oceanic and Atmospheric Administration), an agency of the United States Department of Commerce, and to IGFA (American Gamefish Association) and all of their most cooperative staff of people for generously sharing technical advice and information on specific subjects related to their occupation.

INTRODUCTION

It is the purpose of this book to give in a convenient form a review of my knowledge concerning fishing in saltwater, along the coastlines, offshore, open water, and estuaries and to make the final result of other specialists in the field accessible to those who enjoy and appreciate fishing and the fishes that abound in a saltwater wilderness.

Fishing, as a term, is general, while angling is a special kind of fishing. The word angling is supposed to have been derived from the bend of a hook, forming an angle; but the origin of antiquity of the term is comparatively unimportant now. It is sufficient to know that the art of angling "requires as much enthusiasm as poetry, as much patience as mathematics, and as much caution as housebreaking."

In order to pursue with success any branch of fishing, a knowledge of senses and habits as well as habitats of fishes to be fished, by any method, should be carefully studied. So also should

1

their food. They have their time to eat and their choice of food. It is commonly conceived that fishing is not as good as usual during easterly winds; but this is only true when winds cause the tides to rise so high on the coastlines that fish change their feeding grounds.

When is the best time to fish? Well, I would like to quote an old saying for the diehard: "When the wind is in the east - fish bite the least, when in the west - fishing is at its best, when in the north - fishingpersons go forth, when in the south - the bait floats in the fish's mouth. The best time to fish is when you have the time."

Humankind has always held a special fascination for fish. Perhaps it is because fish belong to a world that is totally unlike ours. Possibly it is because there are so many kinds of fishes that there seem to be endless variations on an ever-changing theme. Perhaps it is because the fish, with its streamline body, its flashing silvery sides, and its brilliant colors, seems so at home and so much in harmony with our universe that we are moved to wonder and perhaps even feel a trace of envy.

Somehow we equate fishing with peace and relaxation in a way that goes beyond the mere anticipation of a pleasant and nutritious meal. Even those who fish for a living seem to reflect an inner serenity as if they absorbed some of the tranquility that fish seem to have. This is often reflected in the language of the fishingperson who never uses the word kill to describe their successes.

SALT WATER FISHING AS A SPORT

Back in the 1800's saltwater fishing with "fancy" tackle (rod and reel) was mostly a rich person's sport. Wealthy sportspersons could afford to belong to exclusive fishing clubs where initiation fees ran up to $1,000. They could also afford to take days off, travel long distances, and buy the best saltwater fishing tackle - usually custom made. The average working person had to use an ordinary handline when fishing in the surf, from piers or boats.

But fishing with handlines wasn't very efficient or productive. One could not cast too far via the "heave and haul" method, and could not work artificial lures very well. And handline fishing didn't provide much fun or sport in fighting a fish.

The picture started to change right after World War I. Booming industries, higher wages, more leisure time and the automobile enabled people to travel to distant areas to go saltwater fishing. And fishing tackle manufacturers started to turn out better rods and reels at prices almost everyone could afford.

Today we have a wide variety of rods, reels, lures, and accessories for sale at our local bait and tackle shops, sporting goods stores, and department stores, or other outlets. Or you can send for the catalogs advertised in many outdoor magazines.

Unlike the hunters who must think like their game to have a successful days hunt, one can never think like a fish. Only after years of study a careful observer can learn his quarry's habits and can anticipate the fish's movements and responses but no mere human can ever know the sensations of vibrations striking a *lateral line.

Until the middle of this century most people took it for granted that fish as well as other living resources of the sea were limitless.

Hadn't commercial fishingpersons been harvesting tuna in huge fish traps since the earliest days of the Christian era? Hadn't northern European seafarers been taking cod from the Grand Banks since before Columbus sighted San Salvador? But as the fish-catching ability of maritime nations grew at an explosive rate following World War II, it became apparent that many species of fish were in danger of following certain land-dwelling mammals and bird species into virtual extinction. Inland in the narrow confines of fresh water rivers and lakes it is easy to observe the effects of overfishing, pollution, and the destruction of habitat on vunerable species. However, much is being done about rectifying this problem by our local Game and Fresh Water Fish Commission, and Federal agencies as well as members of our many fine fishing clubs. Because of the confined areas it is much easier to control the freshwater situation because of state laws. But to accomplish this in the salty seas suddenly becomes a big problem.

Against conservation of species and habitat to endangered marine fishes of the oceans is the fact that on the high seas, beyond territorial limits, the fish belong to everybody. Therefore, it requires the help of all nations to regulate over-fishing or misuse of marine environment. Today, many countries are learning and finally agreeing on what constitutes conservation of marine species. Much has already been done by our National Marine Fisheries Service, NOAA (NationalOceanic and Atmospheric Administration, U.S. Department of Commerce) in preventing the overfishing of mackerel, redfish, red snapper, snook, etc.

Through its lateral line a fish can determine directions in currents of water, detect the presence of nearby objects through variations in water pressure, and also sense vibrations. This ability is useful to a fish in navigating at night or in murky waters, in keeping schooling fish together, and also in locating food and escaping predators. Lateral lines are distinctly shaped and of various lengths and are important sensory organs. All fish have a lateral line or two. (See illustration on the bottom of page 58).

SALT VS FRESH WATER FISHING

Usually when an angler, experienced in the ways of fresh water and its inhabitants makes his or her first contact with saltwater they go about it timidly, for even the water itself doesn't seem to look, or act the same as it does inland. In addition, with such awesome expanses to look upon, the proposition becomes more than confusing. Where should an angler put down his or her line? Where are the fish going to be.

The fact is, saltwater is different in the way it "acts". But at the same time many of the complex influences which have important bearing upon the catching of fish in freshwater will also apply in the oceans. For example, if water temperature is either too high or too low, fish become listless, no matter what kind of water they inhabit. Wind direction which may muddy or cool the water will also inhibit fish. A falling barometer generally causes fish to lie close to bottom and bite poorly, while a rising barometer will usually accentuate activity again; low or high oxygen content makes fish listless or active respectively.

It is all of these complex influences acting together, and many more thrown in, that makes fishing the wonderfully exciting game it is. But there is another influence that may possibly be stronger than all of these, in both fresh and salt water, and especially so in the latter. This is the tidal pull of the moon. The pull of the tidal influence is just as strong inland, but the bodies of water are too small to be appreciably affected as far as what we see is concerned. This tidal pull undoubtedly influences the activity of fish. In saltwater, however, the tides, which we can actually see, govern directly much of the activity of all marine life, not alone by the mysterious moon pull, but far more by the action of currents and by the lowering and raising the water levels several times each full day.

Therefore, to be a successful saltwater angler, one must understand this great influence. It is as important as the tackle one chooses. It is an interesting subject in itself, and related to angling, it will actually govern the size of the catch, almost without fail. In other words, the salty angler must plan his or her fishing in relation to the tides.

The terminology and explanation are as follows:

incoming tide - toward shore

high tide - crest of incoming tide

outgoing tide - away from shore

low tide - minimum low water level of outgoing tide

The varying water levels caused by the tides radically shift and change feeding conditions for fish, closing off or opening up new feeding grounds, covering and uncovering food, forcing forage fish to move, changing shallow water, and beach contours. There are two low tides, two high tides each full day, roughly six hours apart.

Tides are actually caused by the pull of both sun and moon. The moon pull is strongest. A "moon (lunar) or tidal day" is almost an hour longer than a "sun (solar) day." Therefore, each day every tide is a little later, and some days therefore do not have four tides.

Most newspapers in coastal towns and cities print tide tables (times) daily. The wise angler will follow them. ⟶

Tides cause currents. "Flood tide" means a shoreward current - an "ebb tide," an offshore current. A "slack tide" means a maximum high, or low, therefore no current. "Tide rips" are caused where opposing currents, brought about by quick depth changes, or shore contours, oppose each other.

As a rule, fish feed most avidly on an incoming tide, retiring to deeper water on an outgoing tide. From an hour before high tide to an hour after is generally the peak of the feeding period. Currents and tide rips stir up food along shoals, bars, inlets, passes, and are therefore hot spots for shore or near-shore anglers. Also, the half-hour to hour immediately following slack tide, either low or high, usually sets the fish feeding, for the new water movement, whether inshore or offshore, stirs up food and causes small forage fish to move. Knowing these facts of saltwater fishing, an angler will have won the first battle in filling his or her live box or stringer as well as assuring themselves of hair raising, unequalled sport. After learning all about the tides in relation to fishing saltwater, the angler must also learn the different kinds of fish he or she may catch. As well as their dominating influences.

ST. PETERSBURG TIMES
tides for Sunday, November 27, 1988

	High	Low	High	Low
St. Petersburg	2:28a	11:11a	....	....
Anna Maria	12:21a	8:40a	....	....
Apalachicola	4:28a	1:55p	....	....
Bayport	1:56a	9:56a	4:14p	9:12p
Boca Grande	1:16a	9:15a	....	....
Bradenton	1:04a	10:16a	....	....
Carrabelle	3:03a	11:42a	....	....
Cedar Key	2:26a	10:08a	4:44p	9:24p
Clearwater	12:35a	8:31a	2:53p	7:47p
St. Petersburg Beach Cswy	1:10a	10:27a	....	....
Courtney Campbell Pkwy	4:03a	1:01p	....	....
Cortez	12:28a	9:46a	....	....
Dunedin, St. Joseph Sound	12:33a	8:21a	2:51p	7:37p
Egmont Key	12:01a	8:47a	....	....
Englewood	1:31a	10:31a	....	....
Gandy Bridge	3:35a	12:37p	....	....
Gulfport	12:56a	10:06a	....	....
Hillsborough Bay	2:35a	11:37a	....	....
Indian Rocks	1:26a	9:13a	3:44p	8:29p
Johns Pass	12:14a	9:07a	....	....
Little Manatee River	2:28a	11:11a	....	....
Madeira Beach Cswy	12:48a	9:53a	....	....
Naples	12:56a	8:34a	3:14p	7:50p
Pass A Grille	12:54a	9:41a	....	....
Pinellas Point	2:06a	10:42a	....	....
Placida	1:01a	10:12a	....	....
Punta Gorda	3:34a	12:38p	....	....
Punta Rassa	1:27a	9:52a	....	....
St. Marks River Entrance	2:55a	10:38a	5:13p	9:54p
Safety Harbor	4:06a	1:06p	....	....
Sarasota	12:50a	10:13a	....	....
Skyway Mullet Key Ent	12:06a	9:13a	....	....
Steinhatchee River Ent	2:40a	10:35a	4:58p	9:51p
Suwanee River Entrance	2:29a	10:24a	4:47p	9:40p
Tarpon Springs, Anclote River	1:35a	9:25a	3:53p	8:41p
Venice	12:26a	9:33a	....	....
Withlacoochee River Ent	2:30a	11:01a	4:48p	10:17p

Tomorrow's Key Tides

	High	Low	High	Low
St. Petersburg	3:22a	11:57a	....	....
St. Marks River Entrance	3:33a	11:21a	5:59p	10:43p

To compute tomorrow's tides, determine how much earlier or later than the key tide (St. Petersburg or St. Mark's) the tide is today at your point of interest. Tomorrow's tide will be the same amount of time earlier or later.

Gulf water temperature at Egmont Key 73 degrees.

7

SALT WATER TACKLE AND HOW TO USE IT
FOR YOUR FAVORITE METHOD OF FISHING

Methods of fishing in salt water are no different than those used in fresh water fishing; only the tackle is different. The following suggestions for tackle to use for your favorite way of fishing is outlined as a starting point. However, once you get the feel of things it is up to you, the angler, to select the most suitable tackle that will enable you to fish with comfort and yet be able to handle anything that challenges you.

SALT WATER BAIT CASTING TACKLE

Bait casting is usually described as the technique of casting an artificial bait or lure with a revolving-spool reel. Actually, this definition requires a bit of qualification. In reality the bait casting rod and reel are specialized developments that are designed to cast artificial lures or baits to specific kinds of fish. From the early prototypes to the present machine-age equipment many changes, all improvements, have been made. The modern bait casting reel, for instance, is a descendent of those first perfected by Kentucky jewelers as early as 1810. Present reels have the star drag and free-spool devices, and many are equipped with level-wind devices, and many have an antibacklash device built into the reel. The great appeal of bait casting tackle is its versatility. A good quality outfit may be used for casting, trolling, live bait or bottom fishing. However, although your good fresh water bait casting tackle can be used in salt water it is definitely not advisable because all tackle should be rust proof and mineral resistant due to the fact that salt water is very corrosive

SALT WATER BAIT CASTING RODS

The length of the bait casting rod will depend on the kind of fishing you will do, the weight of the lures or live bait cast, and whether you fish from a boat, from the shoreline, or wading a flat or shallow area. Many salt-water anglers fishing confined creeks and narrow canals, lined with trees or brush will usually use a short salt water rod that allows easier casting among such shoreline obstacles; the same holds true for the angler casting the same area from a boat. However, when casting from open shorelines or wading, longer rods are preferred, those with a limber action to cast lighter artificials and work them properly. The rods used by salt water anglers have a longer butt section or handle.

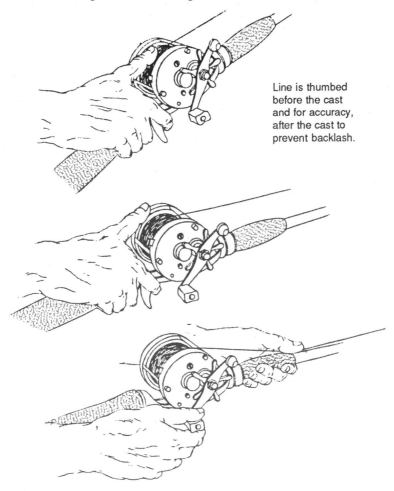

Line is thumbed before the cast and for accuracy, after the cast to prevent backlash.

SALT WATER BAIT CASTING REELS

Many salt water anglers use a conventional free spool bait casting reel that is equipped with a level-wind mechanism and a lever or button that enables them to disengage gears so that the spool turns but the handle remains stationary during the cast which

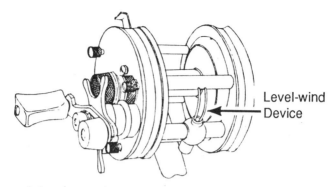

Level-wind Device

helps somewhat to produce smoother, longer casts. Many of the reels may also be equipped with an anti-backlash device that can be adjusted to coincide with the weight of your artificial or natural bait.

When purchasing a reel for use for salt water fishing, make sure that it is made of a non corrosive metal.

SALT WATER BAIT CASTING ARTIFICIALS

Saltwater artificial baits are very similar to the fresh water kinds. There are, however, plugs made for salt water fishing that offer resistance to salt water corrosion. There are spoons of various kinds up to 1 1/2 or 2 ounces that are used for catching many different species of fish. When trolling, the lighter spoons are more popular, but for casting, the heavier are better. Action of spoons is changed by the speed used in retrieving them.

There are jigs made of bucktail, feathers, or nylon skirts, all are proven fish getters and can be successfully used to catch striped bass, weakfish (seatrout), tarpon, snook, Spanish and King mackerel as well as many other species. Jigs weighing 1/2 ounce upwards to 2 ounces are ideal for bait casting. Plugs of the popping kinds, and swimming, and crippled minnow types are very effective in salt water on fish species that prey on smaller fish that they chase on the surface.

There are also many underwater artificials that are of the natural minnow kinds that come in silver and a wide variety of

10

combinations of colors, and some are with different kinds of metal lips that create action and even deep diving, and then there are some that are straight and have to be worked into desired actions with the fishing rod tip.

And last, but not least, the ever popular plastic worms and eels are also used to catch salt water fish, as are some plastic jigs of many shapes.

HOW TO FIND BAIT CASTING GROUNDS

For the saltwater casting angler, from the waters edge or a boat just offshore are ideal areas for the angler using conventional bait casting or spin casting tackle with light-weight qualities. Bays, sounds, estuaries, and brackish water rivers are ideal for this kind of fishing. Another area that is good and easy to reach is the tidal creeks that wind in, through, and out of the saltwater marshlands. Here the angler fishes close to any undercut bank or deep hole, especially during the early mornings and at dusk during the incoming tide.

Another good area to fish is where a river empties into the ocean. Gamefish of many kinds usually wait for an incoming tide to bring their meals of shrimp, crabs and baitfish.

Bridges spanning inlets and channels as well as small, but deep creeks. In these places one can fish from the structure or from the shoreline or use a boat close enough to enable you to cast close to the banks.

Just remember that anywhere you choose to fish, always fish during, and one hour after an incoming tide. The reason being that many of the areas just described are usually uncovered during the low tide period and all fish will move in to feed during the incoming tide.

11

SURF CASTING

Surf casting is somewhat identical with fresh water bait or plug casting, except that with such heavy tackle both hands are used for making the cast. However, the long rod butt makes this possible. The cast is usually begun with the angler standing either close to the water's edge or ankle deep in the surf. Like fresh water bait casting, the overhead cast is the most popular and the most used.

SURF FISHING RODS

In choosing a surf rod it is important to know where you will be fishing most of the time. Will it be from a sandy beach, rocky shore, jetty or other location? Most beginners choose a spinning surf rod because it is easier to use and cast with them than the conventional types. Spinning surf rods can be broken down into three classes; light, medium and heavy. The light spinning surf rod will run from 7 1/2 to 9 feet. It is used with the smaller spinning reels, and 10, 12, or 15 pound test lines to cast lures up to two ounces. The medium-weight rod runs from 8 to 10 feet. It is used with larger spinning reels filled with 15 or 20 pound test line to cast lures up to 3 ounces. This rod is best for "all-around" fishing from the beach, rocky shores or jetties. The heavy spinning surf rod runs

10 to 14 feet and is used with a heavy-duty spinning reel loaded with 20 to 30 pound test lines and will cast lures up to 4 or 5 ounces. This rod is good for big fish, long casts, and for bait fishing with heavy sinkers. Surf rods come in one piece or two sections. The longer one-piece rods must be transported outside the car. Two piece rods break down and can be carried inside the car or trunk.

REELS

Conventional surf reels have a revolving spool, free-spool lever, star-drag; for best results they must be thumbed during the cast. They are still used by some surf anglers for big fish and bait fishing, but surf spinning reels are more popular today and are definitely best for the beginner. The open-faced surf spinning reels

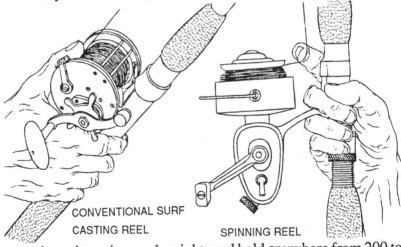

CONVENTIONAL SURF
CASTING REEL   SPINNING REEL

come in various sizes and weights and hold anywhere from 200 to 400 yards of line, depending on the pound test the angler prefers. Small sized surf reels are used with light surf spinning rods; larger reels with medium rods, and the biggest reels with the heaviest surf rods. An ideal combination for all surf casting is a medium/heavy action rod, 9 feet in length that will cast a 1.4 ounce lure or live bait with ease; reel should be a spinning reel that is with a gear ratio of 4.3:1. Line should be monofilament with a test of 15 or 20 pounds. Lures upwards to 3 ounces may be used with this rig.

LINES

Monofilament lines testing 20 to 45 pounds, can be used on a conventional reel. For surf spinning reels, monofilament lines testing from 10 to 30 pounds are used, with lighter lines best for light tackle, small fish, and light lures. For big fish, heavy lures and when fishing in rocky areas or in heavy surf and strong currents, a 20 or even 40 pound test line can be used.

SURF RIGS

For bait fishing in the surf, two rigs are popular. One is the standard rig where the hook on the leader is tied to a three-way swivel a few inches above the sinker. The other is the "fish-finder rig" where a ring and snap moves up and down the line; the snap holds the sinker and the line is threaded through the ring (as illustrated). A barrel swivel acts as a stop for the sinker and the leader and hook are tied to the swivel. Pyramid sinkers weighing from 3 to 5 ounces, depending on weight of rod, are usually used with a medium to heavy action surf rod when fishing sandy beaches. In rocky areas you can use bank or round sinkers, available in many weights.

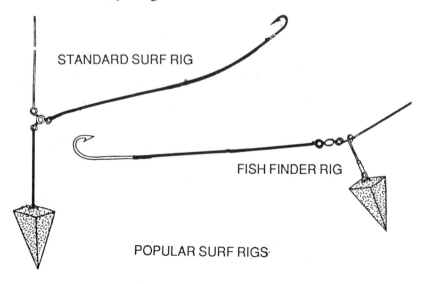

STANDARD SURF RIG

FISH FINDER RIG

POPULAR SURF RIGS

SURF "SHOCK LEADER" TO LINE KNOT

1. When leader is five times or more the pound/test of line, double ends of both leader and line back about 6 inches. Slip loop of line through loop of leader far enough to permit tying Uni-Knot around both strands of leader.

2. With doubled line, tie Uni-Knot around the two strands of leader. Use only four turns.

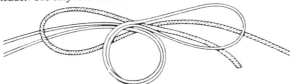

3. Put finger through loop of line and grasp both tag end and standing line to pull knot snug around loop of leader.

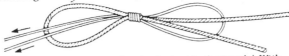

4. With one hand pull standing leader (not both strands). With other hand pull both strands of line (see arrows). Pull slowly until knot slides to end of leader loop and all slippage is gone.

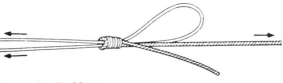

Surgeon's End Loop

Use this knot to tie a loop in the end of a line for attaching leaders or other terminal tackle quickly.

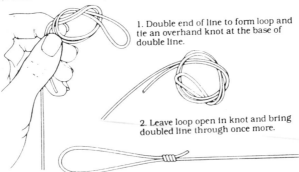

1. Double end of line to form loop and tie an overhand knot at the base of double line.

2. Leave loop open in knot and bring doubled line through once more.

3. Hold standing line and tag end and pull loop to tighten knot. Size of loop can be determined by pulling loose knot to desired point and holding it while knot is tightened. Clip tag end.

MAKING THE SURF CAST

Surf casting is somewhat identical to bait casting, except that with such heavy tackle both hands must be used in making the cast. The long rod handles or butt makes this possible. The cast is begun with the angler standing either close to the water's edge or perhaps ankle-deep in the surf. The angler faces parallel to the shoreline, with rod tip pointing shoreward, the rod held about mid-chest high and at almost right angles to his or her body, the tip dipping slightly. The right hand grips the butt near the reel (which is placed near top of the butt), thumb upon the reel spool. The left hand grips the far end of the rod butt. By keeping the hands widely spaced, greater power of swing, therefore greater distance of cast, is possible. The sinker and bait, or casting lure, is allowed to lie on the sand with a couple of feet of line between it and rod tip, until cast is made.

Making the cast now requires nothing but a powerful up-and-over swing, thumb holding the reel spool firmly until the rod has reached almost a vertical position. The reel is then released, the bait and sinker travels high and swiftly out over the waves. Meanwhile, the angler follows through with the rod, swinging the right leg around so that, as the bait hits the water, he or she is facing the spot where it landed, angler's back to the shore. The surf casting method of casting just described is for a free-spooling conventional reel. For spin-casting in the surf, hold the rod with the right hand at the reel seat with the thumb on top and the other fingers below (as illustrated). Two fingers can be placed in front of the leg or support of the reel and two behind. Left hand holds the rod butt. With the bailer pulled down and back into the lock position, with your left hand turn the reel handle until the line roller is on top; then pick up the line with the index finger of the right hand. Then back off the reel handle so that the line is freed from the roller, after which the left hand pushes the wire bail down until it locks in the casting postion. Bring the rod up to the shoulder height with reel

When using a conventional Reel thumb must hold line spool at the beginning of cast.

Bailer is in locked position and the angler is holding the line with forefinger of the reel hand (left).

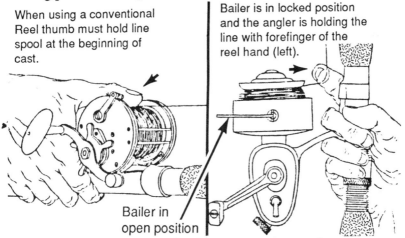

Bailer in open position

facing up. Next, with a quick motion, bring the rod tip up over your head. The tip will bend in an arc and then start to propel the bait forward, at which time you release the line from your finger and bring the rod down with the tip pointing toward the target. When the bait reaches the target, bring your finger down to the lip of spool to stop your cast. Timing is the most important factor in casting along with the "feel" of the weight of the bait or sinker. Release the bailer, crank in excess slack and you are ready to experience one of the greatest methods of saltwater fishing.

A surf belt, a leather belt with a heavy leather cup, to receive the butt of the rod, is a must for the surf angler, especially should one be angling for large stripers or a shark. Another must is a spike, or rod holder for when you still-fish with live bait in the surf - the most popular, easiest and most effective method in general. There are several types of rod holders. The spike is a steel rod, or flattened steel band usually about three feet in length, sharpened on one end so it can be shoved deep down into the sand. On the other end there is an aperature, or iron ring, or other device into which the rod butt may be slipped and solidly held. Thus, after the cast, the rod can be slipped into the spiked top. This eases the work for the angler and serves to hold the rod up high, which keeps the line out of the wash of the breakers. By watching the rod tip, the angler can tell the instant a strike is made. The angler then simply slips the rod out of the holder, sets the hook and drops the rod butt into the belt cup to fight the fish. Surf anglers can make their own rod holder from a flat steel band and a short length of PVC pipe. There are two kinds, any of the two will serve the purpose (see illustration). A suggestion to the angler, when placing the rod holder into the sand, do not place it in an extreme vertical position, but instead slant it backwards a niche (see illustration). I have stood by helplessly as a fish pulled the rod out to sea because the pole holder was slanted seaward and the drag was tightly set on the reel. Another hint is never set the drag too tight, it is best to set it after the fish hits and you pull the rod from the holder and have it tightly in your hands. Of course if you feel that you have everything under control for a big hit, preset your drag and be ready.

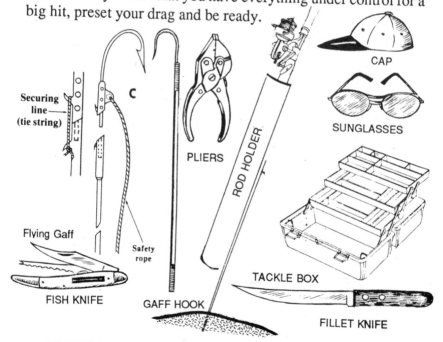

Securing line (tie string)

CAP

SUNGLASSES

C

PLIERS

ROD HOLDER

Flying Gaff

Safety rope

FISH KNIFE

GAFF HOOK

TACKLE BOX

FILLET KNIFE

ACCESSORIES FOR THE SERIOUS ANGLER

SURF FISHING LURES AND BAITS

Heavy spoon-type lures are good as are the assorted metal squids. These are usually made of stainless steel or other metals which are chrome or nickle-plated. Your old casting plugs, large ones, that were used in northern fresh waters are also ideal, surface and diving types including poppers, swimmers, crippled baitfish which moves on the surface creating a commotion. These plugs are ideal for all kinds of fish that feed in the surf; bluefish, redfish, striped bass, etc. When stripers are running and feeding in the shoreline, underwater plugs that dive and travel just below the surface or a few feet below are good, but few artificials can surpass the use of your largest, largemouth bass bait, the plastic worm or eel - they must, however, be not less than ten inches in length and be with an action head that provides casting weight and gives the lure an eel lifelike movement. Eels should be reeled at slow speeds for best results, especially at night when they are most effective. When in the shoreline and are not wearing waders it is best to wear sneakers to protect your feet from getting cuts from broken shell debris as well as protection against the stingrays which have the habit of burying themselves in the sand. A stab or laceration from their spine, on the tail, can be very painful and should be treated immediately with an antiseptic. Should the spine break off in the foot seek medical help at once.

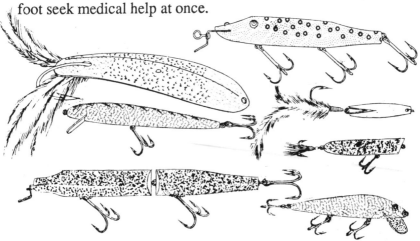

19

SURF CASTING

Bait used in the surf will depend on what you are expecting to catch, and the method used to get it beyond the breakers. Casting will usually limit you to the use of a medium sized mullet, chunk bait or other small baits like shrimp, squid, crab or a large lure. If you want to use a heavier bait you will have to employ some sort of floatation to get the bait into deeper water. A balloon is often used by many surf casters. This is most often used at the beginning of an outgoing tide. However, when using such a floating device it is best to tie a light, possible a two pound test line to connect the balloon line to the top swivel of your bait finder or standard surf rig. This light line comes in handy after your floating device takes your bait out where you want it and then with a hard setting the light line breaks and your bait settles to the bottom.

The proper setting of a hook when fishing in the surf should be done with your rod held parallel to the ground or water, and then with a sharp twist at the waist. This action places your entire body weight, rather than just the strength of your wrist and arms, behind the rod tip. Remember, a sharp hook is always a must.

GLOVES should always be made available for grabbing your line or leader to beach a large fish, however, whenever possible a gaff should be used. A further suggestion for fish weighing more than 25 pounds, a flying-gaff should be used.

LANDING a large fish in a heavy surf is not too easy, but it can be made so by letting the incoming surf work for you. NEVER attempt to drag a large fish through outgoing breakers, such action can snap your line, straighten the hook or tear the fish off the hook. PUMP and CRANK your fish in on each crest of an incoming breaker, but only allow it to slide back on a taught line, with the undertow. When your timing is right you will be able to keep the fish coming on a wave that will eventually beach your fish, high and dry. It is at this time that you either grab the line or leader or drive your gaff home and beach your catch.

CAUTION should be heeded when fishing in the surf!

1. When wading while fishing in a heavy surf, keep your eyes on the incoming breakers, never turn your back to them.

2. Never wade out too far if the breakers are strong, or a great pull of the undertow is obvious.

3. Never wear hip boots - if anything, wear chest-high waders. However, if the surf is warm, long pants or shorts can be worn, however, always wear boat shoes (sneakers) to protect your feet from cuts from rocks and broken seashells and of course, from the spines of a resting stingray or sea urchin.

4. Never tie a stringer of fish to your waist while deep in the surf. This habit can attract sharks and barracudas. Tie your stringer to a long pole stuck deep into the sand or a special rig, close to the beach in about one to two feet of water.

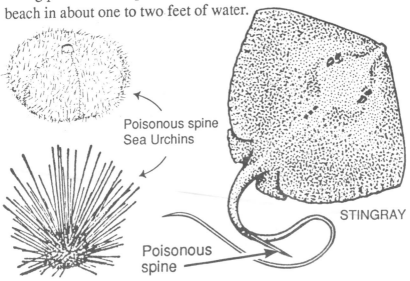

Poisonous spine
Sea Urchins

Poisonous spine

STINGRAY

WHERE TO FISH IN THE SURF

Finding fish or fishing areas along the surf may be rather difficult for the novice angler. Here again, try to locate areas along the beach where other anglers are fishing, if fish are being caught you can join them, but don't get too close as to interfere with their fishing. Many old-timers will ignore you unless you are loud and rowdy and moving all over the beach. On the other hand many local tackle shops will offer help as to a good place to surf cast. However, if you are entirely on your own look for evidence that suggests a productive area, such as the color of the water that usually indicates its depth. For instance, dark blue, dark green usually indicates deep waters, sloughs or channels. Should the water be a light green or brown with stirred up sand, or white with strong wave action, may prove out to be a sand bar or shallow area. When such areas are covered with water, they often have many representatives of the surf fish group that are in season. Strong wave action usually wash out crabs and sand fleas into a slough, the deep area between a sand bar and the beach, and surf fish often occupy the inside of the bar to fed on these crusty crustaceans. Many bars are with cuts and breaks that provide good fishing. Some beaches have rock jetties which are usually spaced at certain intervals - jetties often provide excellent fishing, when bait and rig are layed very close to the rocks or in deep holes formed by a stack of rocks.

SALTWATER TROLLING

Trolling is another popular method for catching fish. Trolling is somewhat comparable to drift fishing by the fact that both methods allow the angler to cover a lot of ground. Some anglers refer to trolling as the most popular and important saltwater method. For those anglers fortunate enough to own a seaworthy boat or able to afford a charter boat or rent one will be challenged by a great variety of fish species from all depths of the sea. Should the first time out be successful, the Angler is spoiled for life and will resent having to fish by any other method. I myself have been very successful in trolling the seas, but I have also been very successful in surf casting; my choice is "give me a surf when the stripers are running and I will leave trolling to the other anglers, that is unless the dolphins, king mackerel, and billfishes are on a feeding binge."

Trolling in the bays and just offshore with a small boat is often very rewarding. Just be sure that your craft is with safety equipment suggested by the local Coast Guard Squadron.

Many saltwater fish travel in large schools and roam widely. By trolling, one of these huge schools can usually be located. Or, for those large saltwater prizes which are solitary travelers, trolling amounts to the same thing as big game hunting. It is like stalking big game fish.

Trolling near the surface is the most popular, for it is easiest and eliminates the use of exceedingly large sinkers, which would otherwise be necessary to get the bait or lure down to great depths. And nearly all saltwater gamefish which are commonly taken by trolling can be found at some time of day, or tide, near the surface.

Small boat trolling in bays, lagoons, channels, etc., differs in no way from fresh water trolling. The lure, or natural bait, is simply tossed overboard and allowed to run out some distance behind the boat. With artificials, such as plugs, etc., it is common in saltwater, either in casting or trolling, to give the rod a long sweep, or jerk, every couple of seconds (in casting, this is done by jerking the rod tip then reeling in the slack caused by such rod action, and continually repeating the process. The motion caused by the jerking of the rod tip is transferred to the lure which presents lifelike action that is particularly deadly for most saltwater fish.

For open-water trolling after larger saltwater gamefish, there are several differences for regulation trolling.

Flat trolling is one method. It means you troll by the usual method, sitting at the stern of the boat, holding the rod, letting the line run straight back. This has many disadvantages. It means only one person at a time can successfully work a line in open water. It is back-breaking work, when you must hold heavy tackle against the pull of the long, heavy line and bait. It is difficult to fashion and hook up bait such as strips of fish or whole fish in such a way that flat trolling won't soon rip them from the hook or tear them to pieces.

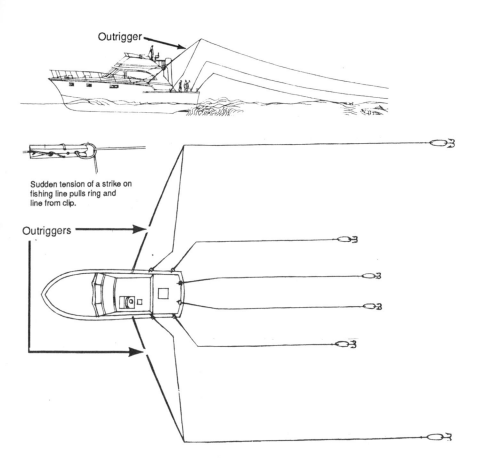

Outrigger

Sudden tension of a strike on
fishing line pulls ring and
line from clip.

Outriggers

Outrigger trolling has therefore been developed (devices used
on all deep-sea charter boats) to overcome the difficulties of deep-
sea flat trolling. The out-rigger is a long pole, several of which are
placed at various angles sticking out and upward from the sides
and stern of the trolling boat. Regular tackle is set up, but the line
from each rod is held to the end of an outrigger by a wooden clothes
clip and held high in the air, and the bait, far behind, is made to skip
enticingly along the surface by adjusting the speed of the boat.
When a strike comes, the line is yanked from its outrigger holder,
the angler grabs the rod, sets the hook, and the fight is on. Several
trollers are able to fish simultaneously from the same boat without
getting fouled. There is less water pull on the line, less wear and
tear on the angler and bait.

FOUR POPULAR SALTWATER
DEEP TROLLING METHODS

There are, at the present time, four popular methods or systems being used by saltwater anglers. All work very well, and are very productive. They are:

1. The so-called multiple-depth, multiple lure system which includes the use of a heavy fixed weight and any number of artificials and natural baits.

2. The expendable-weight drip-sinker system.

3. The fish-planer, or what is referred to as a paravane system.

4. The fast becoming popular down-rigger system.

Of four methods only 1, 2, and 3 systems are utilized without wire fishing lines; in system 4 a wire fishing line may be used. However, all four systems may be trolled with the use of a motor driven boat, and except for the down rigger method all call for the use of common, conventional tackle, only the down rigger requires the use of elaborate tackle.

Depth of bait on all systems is controlled by length of fishing line trailing the boat, the planer sometimes calls for more line and/ or faster boat speed.

THE MULTIPLE DEPTH SYSTEM: Here the fishing line must be at least a medium trolling line with a 30 to 40 pound breaking test. All hardware live swivels, snaps, etc. should be made of brass. Brass swivel should be placed between sections separating the branch lines, usually separated at 9 to 18 foot intervals. Branch lines are made of main line material which should be between 10 to 30 feet in length (as illustrated). Tackle, such as rod reel and main line, must be heavy enough to control and support several pounds of rigged tackle, bait included, and of course one, two or more fighting fish.

This multiple depth method is very effective in that it permits the angler to cover and explore considerable depths of water levels. Its origin is linked with commercial fishing person, and because of this an angler should check with local authorities

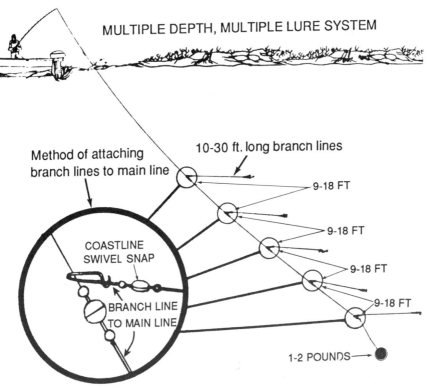

Method of attaching
branch lines to main line

10-30 ft. long branch lines

9-18 FT

9-18 FT

9-18 FT

9-18 FT

COASTLINE
SWIVEL SNAP

BRANCH LINE
TO MAIN LINE

1-2 POUNDS

governing saltwater deep trolling before utilizing the rig, some areas outlaw its use wherever deep trolling is allowed.

TACKLE USED IN THE MULTIPLE DEPTH SYSTEM: Use a 1 to 2 pound ball, dipsey or sand fixed sinker. Use brass snap-swivel may be used for attaching baited hooks or lure; spoons, spinners, and wooden or plastic lures. When using lures it is suggested that a lightweight surface plug be secured to the upper-most branch-line, and the bottom branch-line a diving lure be attached. Spinners and spoons may be used on the remaining in-between branches. Troll at a slow speed when using this rig. Last, but not least, if unfamiliar with the ocean's bottom, a release-sinker device may be utilized so that there is less chance of losing your entire rig should the sinker get hung up on a rock or underwater marine debris. (See release sinker device that follows the planer rig).

27

THE EXPENDABLE-WEIGHT DEEP TROLLING RIG:
Like the planer rig this system allows only one artificial or natural
bait to be used on a line. However, the big advantage here is that
when a fish is hooked the weight of the heavy sinker is removed
from the line, making fishing much more enjoyable and less wear
and tear on the angler and tackle. Weight used is usually a ball
sinker which is with a wire eye that can be conveniently attached
to the sinker release device, however a heavy sand (pyramid) or
dipsey sinker (each with a wire eye) may be used.

THE EXPENDABLE-WEIGHT DROP SINKER SYSTEM

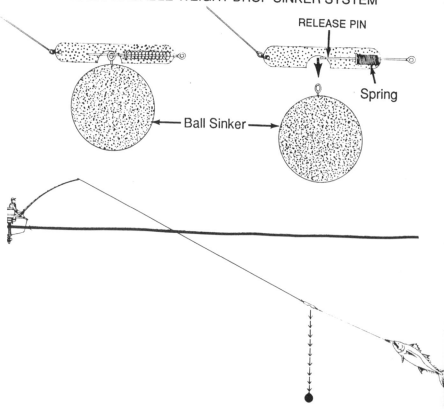

THE EXPENDABLE WEIGHT SINKER RELEASE DE-
VICE: A sinker-release may be used in almost all trolling rigs. A
commercial sinker release may be purchased, or one can make use
of the self-rigged sinker release illustrated on page 38. The

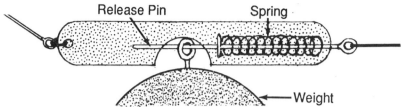

Release Pin   Spring

Weight

commercial device is made of a metal or plastic cylinder with an
eye on each end for connecting the main line, and an internal spring
and sliding pin designed to hold a ball sinker, the most popular
sinker utilized by the serious trolling angler, which is with a wire
eye molded into it, that slips onto the release pin. When a strike
occurs the sudden added line tension pulls back the release pin and
the sinker falls to the bottom and gives the angler a free line to play
the fish and land it. In an emergency many anglers use a large
dipsey, or a sand sinker, both are with a wire eye for convenience.

THE PLANER RIG: This method of trolling involves a metal
or plastic diving device that is with a heavy, well designed towing
yoke (as illustrated) which is attached to the main line with a ball
bearing snap swivel and the baited trail-line is connected to the
other end of the planer with a coastlock swivel snap. The two snaps
used should be of heavy, good quality brass

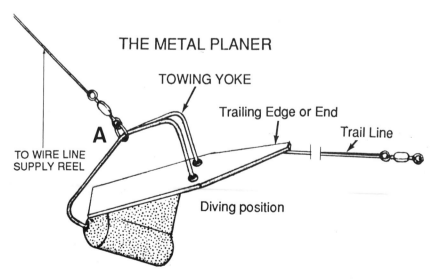

THE METAL PLANER

TOWING YOKE

Trailing Edge or End

Trail Line

A

TO WIRE LINE
SUPPLY REEL

Diving position

29

FISH PLANER SYSTEM

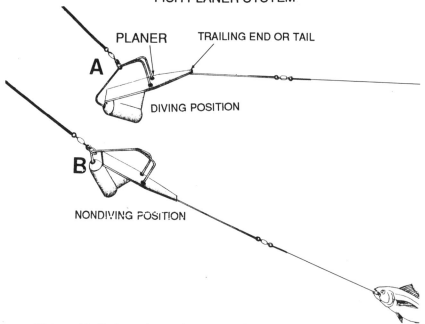

PLANER   TRAILING END OR TAIL

A

DIVING POSITION

B

NONDIVING POSITION

This self diving planer is placed in the fishing line, usually about 15 to 30 feet ahead of the trolling artificial or natural bait. When the planer is in the diving position (A) it is designed to dive as it is being pulled through the water. When tripped into a non-diving position by a striking fish (B), the planer offers little resistance when reeling the fish to gaff.

Many anglers use a planer in a different way, by attaching a line-release device, such as that used with a downrigger (as illustrated below), to the trailing edge or tail of the planer. The depth of the planer depends on the speed of the boat and the amount of the trailing line, the latter being more trustworthy for trolling should be done at slow to moderate speeds when using a planer.

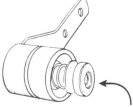

Line Release Device as used in a Downrigger

OPERATING THE PLASTIC ECONOMY PLANER

1. Attach your rod line to the trip line swivel.

2. Attach 3 to 7 feet of leader to tail line swivel.

3. Attach desired lure.

4. Set a starboard course for your Dipper Diver by turning the control tab to the right (Fig. 1). To direct the Big Dipper Diver to run port side turn the control tab to the left (Fig. 2). Send the diver downward by positioning the control tab below the weight and tail (Fig. 3).

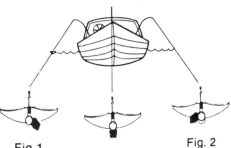

Fig. 1

Fig. 2

Fig. 3

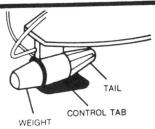
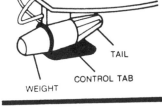

TAIL

CONTROL TAB

WEIGHT

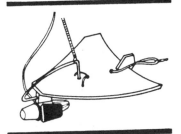

5. You should now be able to trip your Big Dipper by pulling your rod forward without jerking.

6. You may set and unset the Big Dipper in the water by moving the rod forward—to unset and then dropping the rod tip back — to reset.

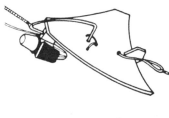

7. Big Dipper Diver will unset itself if it strikes the bottom.

8. Sensitivity setting for the Big Dipper Diver are diagramed below.

9. Trip and reset and repeat to allow flutter trolling at any length. →

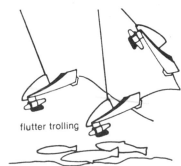

flutter trolling

31

DEEP-TROLLING WITH THE DOWNRIGGER

The downrigger is, in reality, an underwater outrigger that carries a fishing rig to practically any depth you so desire. Trolling depth with a downrigger is accomplished by a heavy weight of special design that is lowered over the side or stern of a boat, most often on the end of a stainless steel wire line. This wire line is stored on a special hand reel that is usually with some sort of line measuring or revolution-counting device to display exactly how much line is out at any given time.

This method of fishing deep with light lines was first used in freshwater by anglers utilizing them for deep trolling for salmon. Today there is a ready market for saltwater non-corrosive units. Although the basic concept has never really changed, there are, however, additional features - such as electric retrieve and water temperature readouts at the depth being trolled. There are even additional uses for downriggers, such as for holding a chub can or pot on the bottom during a strong current or tide when fishing for groupers and snappers. Unlike a fish line the wire holding the downrigger does not develop a belly, which makes it easy to wind up a heavily weight chum-pot for a refill. So sophisticated are some of the new designs of downriggers that some are equipped with computerized additions, for instance a control pad which allows the angler to not only to enter, but to store and change depths; direct vertical movement of the downrigger weight safely during its retrieval; oscillate the bait, artificial or natural, at different speeds and depths; and always know exactly where the bait is. And all saltwater versions are with materials impervious to saltwater corrosion, booms are usually of made of stainless steel as are the components used with it; bodies are usually of Lexan polycarbonate. Most downriggers come equipped with 400 feet of stainless steel cable, reel, depth meter, and adjustable-angle rod hold, snap swivel and a positive deckplate locking wheel. Booms are usually about 18 inch standard length or standard plus 42 and 66 inches (optional). Many can be upgraded from manual to electric to computerized. There is one late model downrigger that is equipped with an interesting innovation that automatically

DOWNRIGGER TROLLING SYSTEM

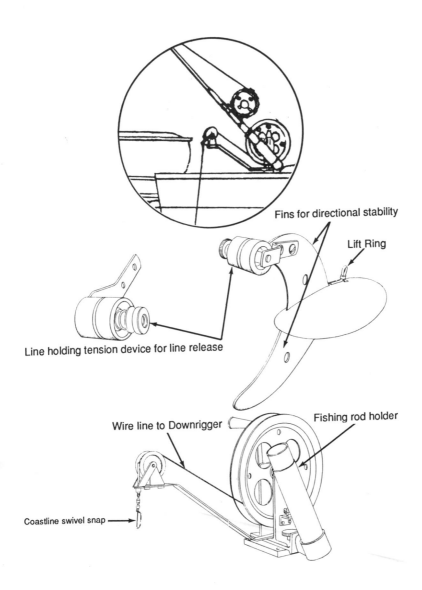

Fins for directional stability

Lift Ring

Line holding tension device for line release

Wire line to Downrigger

Fishing rod holder

Coastline swivel snap

33

provides a forward or upward darting motion to the bait. This model consists of a compact, sealed container with a rod holder on the top.

The weight, of special design, is equipped with an outrigger type of line release. This release may be in the form of a spring-loaded jaw device or a twin-roller device as displayed in the illustration above. In the latter design the line is placed between the rollers after the lure or natural bait is trailing the boat about 20 to 30 feet. At this time both the downrigger weight and fishing line are lowered at the same time to the desired trolling depth which will be recorded on your counting device on the hand reel. This depth may be as little as a few feet below the boat or it may be at the location of a thermocline in much deeper water.

When a fish hits or strikes at the bait, the fishing line is pulled from between the jaws or rollers of the line release device and the angler plays the fish without a heavy annoying conventional sinker. It is at this time that a fishing partner hauls up the downrigger and drops back a baited rig, clips the line into the down riggers line-release device and lowers it to the desired depth while the first fish is being hauled in and the fish below are on a feeding binge.

This all sounds very easy, but fishing with a downrigger calls for the angler to be constantly aware of the depth under the boat. To gain this knowledge quickly and conveniently calls for the use of portable or permanent electronic sounding instrument. A sounder serves at least three primary purposes:

1. It indicates the water depth and the characteristics of the bottom.

2. It indicates fish under the boat.

3. It indicates rocks and other obstructions that must be avoided to prevent damage to the downrigger equipment.

The illustration on the following page displays a hooked fish on the downrigger and a second line being put into the water which will replace the rod in the holder of the downrigger while the hooked fish is being played and landed. Meanwhile the second angler, watching the sounder, observes that the boat is moving over a rocky area. He will quickly reel in some of the downrigger line, lifting the weight above the rocks. The downrigger weight will actually be seen on the screen of the sounding device along with the rocky area.

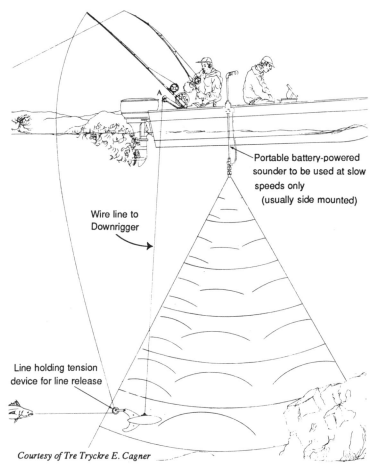

Portable battery-powered sounder to be used at slow speeds only (usually side mounted)

Wire line to Downrigger

Line holding tension device for line release

Courtesy of Tre Tryckre E. Cagner

Downriggers are one of the best advanced methods for trolling which alleviates the use of the old trolling sinkers (the Drail and the Keel) that caused a lot of wear and tear on the tackle as well as the angler (see illustration on page 46).

Downriggers are much more sophisticated than the early ones described above. They are now equipped with an electric motor drive to raise and lower the weights, and with extension rods so that as many as four downriggers can be used, simultaneously, two astern and two over the sides from a single boat. All work very well in depths of more than 165 feet at trolling speeds of under 4 knots. A downrigger weight, usually made of cast iron, weighs between 11 and 15 pounds, and the wire connected usually tests at 75 to 80 pounds.

*(thermocline layer) In general the temperature in the ocean decreases rapidly from the surface downward. Typically there are three layers. There is a mixed or isothermal layer at the surface which may be 60 to 600 feet thick. Below the mixed layer is a thin zone called the thermocline in which there is a rapid drop in temperature. Below the thermocline temperature decreases more gradually.

SUGGESTED TROLLING SPEEDS

(For conventional tackle only, does not include trolling with a planer or downrigger)

SPECIES	SPEED	SPECIES	SPEED
Albacore	4 - 7 mph	Striped Marlin	3 - 6 mph
Amberjack	3 - 5 mph	White Marlin	4 - 7 mph
Barracuda	2 - 4 mph	Sailfish, Atlantic	3 - 5 mph
Striped Bass	2 - 5 mph	Sailfish, Pacific	3 - 5 mph
Bluefish	3 - 4 mph	Weakfish, Spotted	2 - 3 mph
Bonefish	2 - 3 mph	Snook	2 - 3 mph
Cobia	3 - 5 mph	Swordfish	3 - 6 mph
Dolphin (the fish)	4 - 8 mph	Tarpon	2 - 3 mph
Black Drum	3 - 4 mph	Tuna, Bluefin	3 - 7 mph
King Mackerel	3 - 6 mph	Tuna, Yellowfin	4 - 8 mph
Black Marlin	4 - 6 mph	Wahoo	7 - 8 mph
Blue Marlin, Atlantic	4 - 6 mph	Yellowtail, Southern	3 - 5 mph
Blue Marlin, Pacific	5 - 8 mph		

SHARKS ——————

Blue	3 - 5 mph	Hammerhead, Great	3 - 5 mph
Mako	3 - 6 mph	Thresher	3 - 5 mph
Porbeagle	3 - 6 mph	White	2 - 4 mph

Occasionally Tiger sharks are caught while deep trolling at speeds of 3 to 4 mph, which also happens to be an ideal average speed for all species that are usually caught by a trolling system.

WHERE TO TROLL OFFSHORE

Finding fish in a large body of water, like the ocean, is not easy, but nor is it impossible. Before starting out, be sure that your craft is seaworthy to go where you want to fish. And a word of advice before going out on what could wind up to be a "wild" goose chase. Be sure to get as much information about the salt water territory you are about to cover from either local anglers, boaters or consult all the reading material you can digest from local newspapers and magazines and especially from charts, if available. As suggested in the opening of this book, for the first time out, try to hire a guide or charter a small boat, it is well worth it, the big salty sea is not a playground. Your guide will also suggest natural baits, lures, rigs and methods used to catch certain fish. However, should you decide to go it alone, you have to search for fish with binoculars; look for the dark spots, ruffled or rippled surface, slicks, splashes, and floating objects, especially seaweed patches, for under this cover usually swims the tenacious dolphins (the fish). Also look for birds hovering, for when they gather offshore it usually means that large game fish are chasing bait fish to the surface. Frequently you may be able to see baitfish leaping clear of the water during their attempt to escape the jaws of the predators. All disturbances, even the slightest, should be investigated.

Another good bet is to watch for other fishing boats especially those in group and pulling in fish and then try fishing in the general area. Sometimes a large fleet of private boats will be found trolling the same area, chumming and drifting, or even anchored in a particular area. Most offshore anglers use electronic aids that record depths and/or locate fish. And if you have a marine radio tune in because many skippers get on the air and report to others on how they are doing.

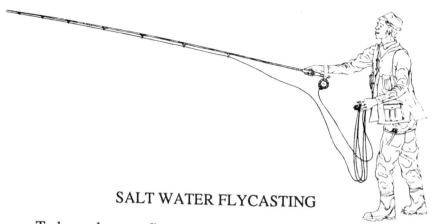

SALT WATER FLYCASTING

Today, salt water flycasting is a sport practiced by many salt water anglers. However, on the whole, it is not a sport for the newly baptized saltwater angler! But it is a fantastically exciting venture for the seasoned freshwater fly fishingperson. Although a regular fresh water fly rod of bass weight may be used it is best to buy a rod that is built for this type of fishing. There are many good salt water fly rods of fiberglass that are equipped with stainless steel guides and anodized aluminum reel seats, which will not corrode in salt water. In fact some manufacturers have gone as far as designing saltwater rods that are with a detachable extension butt that can be added to the end of the rod to provide additional leverage for the angler when fighting a large fish.

It is not surprising to see some of the expert salt water fly anglers challenging the likes of large tarpon, snook, and even some of the bill fishes.

As a general rule, surface flies are usually nowhere near as successful in salt water as they are in fresh water. However, tarpon, striped bass, and a few other species have been known to take them at times. Most types of artificials are in the form of "popping bugs, like or very similar to the large ones used for largemouth bass. The standards that prove most successful for a great variety of salt water fish are the streamer flies in yellows, red, whites, etc. Bucktails in the same colors and metal spinners are excellent as are a variety of spoons.

FLYCASTING REELS

In selecting a salt water fly reel, one must take into consideration that most salt water fish usually caught on fly tackle make longer runs than those caught in fresh water, except for the salmon or steelheads. Therefore, the reel should always be of large capacity and should have plenty of backing line. But here again, manufacturers have designed special reels featuring non-corrosive parts, large line capacity, and a dependable drag. For most of the larger fly rod lures the line will give best results if it is of the "forward taper" (torpedohead) type, of a size and weight, of course, to match rod action and length. Many fly reels are made with a quick release of spool for spare spool change-over from one kind of line to another which allows the angler to build a very versatile line system, ready for everything. Floating lines are considered best for all-round fishing, but sinking lines can also be used when you want your lures to get down deep. The most popular sizes for salt water are WF9F, WF10F, and WF11F.

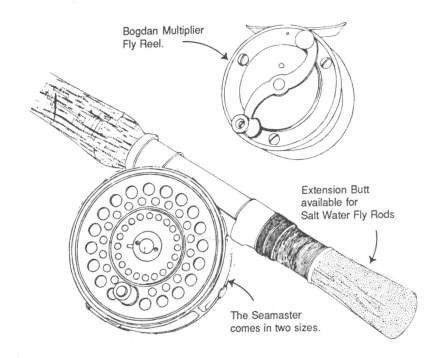

Bogdan Multiplier Fly Reel.

Extension Butt available for Salt Water Fly Rods

The Seamaster comes in two sizes.

FLYCASTING LEADERS

Tapered salt water leaders with 12 pound tippets are tied to the end of the line. For large fish, attach a 12 inch 80 or 100 pound "shock" tippet to the end of the leader.

Like fresh water fly fishing, so be it in salt water; it is most effective on fish that feed in shallow water, such as weakfish (sea trouts), striped bass, bonefish, channel bass (redfish), and snook. However, although seemingly practical for fish running upwards to 20 or 30 pounds, many adept fly anglers have taken tarpon and billfish that weighed upwards to 150 pounds.

SALT WATER FLYCASTING ARTIFICIALS

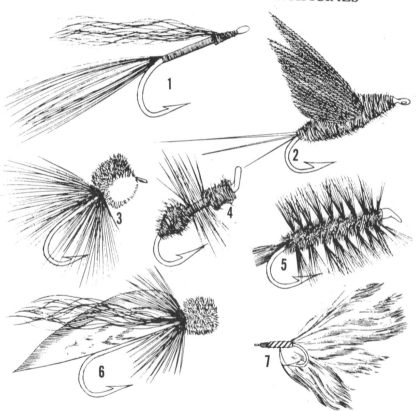

Seven of the most popular salt water flies are displayed above. 1. Keel Hook Fly, 2. Fanwing (dry), 3. Bubble Pup, 4. Ant, 5. Wooly Worm (wet), 6. Mudder Minnow, 7. Marabou.

BOTTOM FISHING

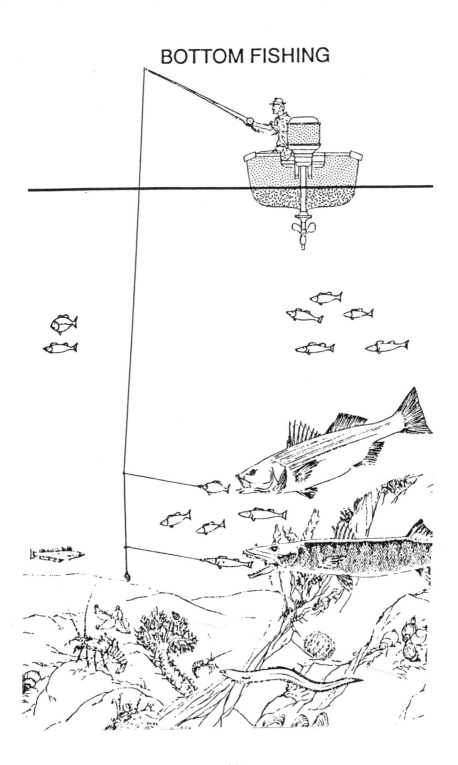

BOTTOM FISHING RODS

Bottom fishing is done from shore, bridges, piers, small boats, private boats, and charter and party boats. Most of the bottom fishing rods are referred to as "pier" or "boat" rods. They range from about 5 to 7 feet in length and are made of solid or hollow glass. The hollow or tubular rods are lighter than solid glass.

For light bottom fishing in shallow and protected bays, sounds, rivers, and inlets for small or medium sized fish, the shorter, lighter bay rods can be used. They are about 5 to 6 feet long and have limber tips. You use them with smaller saltwater reels, lighter lines, and sinkers up to 2 - 4 ounces.

For general bottom fishing from shore, piers, and boats, a rod about 6 or 7 feet long is best. Those with a light or limber action can be used with light lines and sinkers for small fish. But for large fish in deep water, or when fishing in strong currents or tides around rocks and wrecks, a heavy action rod is better. It must be able to handle sinkers upward to 10 ounces.

Some anglers also use surf rods and reels, spinning rods and reels and even some of the trolling or offshore rods. Surf rods, for example, are often used when fishing from piers or even boats when casting is required. Saltwater off-shore trolling or big game rods are used to catch big grouper, jewfish, or black sea bass.

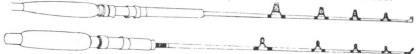

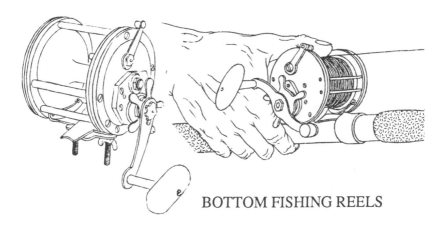

BOTTOM FISHING REELS

Reels used for bottom fishing are usually the conventional "pier," and "boat" saltwater models which work well with most of the lighter bottom rods. But when you are using the heavier bottom fishing rods for big fish in deep water, you often need larger reels. Here many bottom fishingpersons use conventional surf reels and the smaller "trolling," "big game" or "offshore" reels. Sizes No. 3/0, or 4/0 are the most popular since they hold more of the 30, 40, 50 and even 60 pound test lines needed. Most of the bottom fishing reels have a metal spool, drag or brake, and free-spool lever.

BOTTOM FISHING LINES

Years ago bottom fishingpersons used mostly linen lines, then they changed to braided nylon and Dacron lines. Some anglers still like to use Dacron lines when fishing in deep water because they have less stretch. But most anglers going bottom fishing today use monofilament lines. These are smaller in diameter, strong, and are less visible to the fish. When fishing for the smaller fish up to 4 or 5 pounds, you can use lines testing from 10 to 20 pounds. For larger fish up to 20 or 30 pounds, use lines testing from 20 to 30 pounds. And for still bigger bottom fish over coral reefs or wrecks in deep water, use 40 to 50 and even 60 to 80 pound test lines.

HOOKS

Hook patterns used for bottom fishing will depend on the species you are going after; sizes will be governed by the size of the fish running in the area. One of the most popular hooks for bottom fishing is the "claw" or "beak" type hook which has a rolled-in offset point. The old-time Sproat hook is still popular for small and medium sized fish such as sea bass, porgies, sheepshead, croakers, spot, perch, rockfish, and similar species. The Carlisle hook is a long-shank pattern which is good for fish that swallow a bait or have sharp teeth. Use it for eels, flounder or fluke, small bluefish, and silver hake or whiting. Another old-time favorite is the O'Shaughnessy pattern which is forged or flattened to give it strength. It can be used for large bottom fish such as cod, pollock, grouper, halibut, cabezone, and lingcod. Then there are specialized hook patterns such as the Chestertown, which is used for flounders, and the Virginia, used for blackfish or tautog and sheepshead. You can buy hooks already tied on snells or short leaders, and on rigs. They also come loose in a various quantities so you can tie your own leaders and rigs.

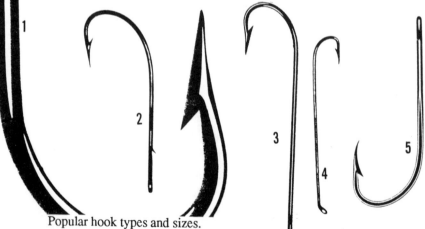

Popular hook types and sizes.
1. Mustad Shark Hook: sizes 6" to 1", 2. Mustad Sproat Hook: sizes 6/0 to 3/0, 3. Superior Carlisle: sizes 10/0 to 20, 4. Mustad Hollow Point Point Flounder Hook: sizes 2 to 10, 5. Mustad Beak Hook: sizes 9/0 to 6, 8, 10, 12. More hook types and sizes continued on page 45.

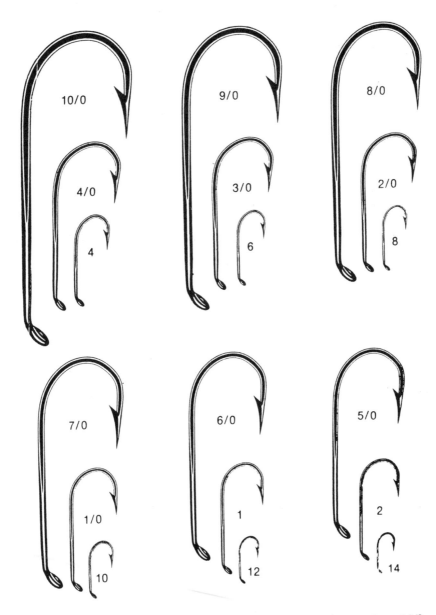

This page displays hook sizes ranging from 14 (very small) to 10/0 (medium large). All are typical of similar sizes in most types, styles and models of hooks.

The above display is adapted with permission from a chart prepared by O. Mustad & Son, Oslo, Norway.

SINKERS

Sinkers are very important in bottom fishing because they get the bait and rig down to the bottom and either hold it there or let it bounce along the bottom. The most popular saltwater bottom sinker is the bank type, which is a long, narrow sinker with several sides and an eye. It comes in weights of 1/2 ounce up to 16 ounces. The diamond sinker is a flat type of weight which is popular with bottom anglers going after fish in deep water. The ball or round sinker is a good one to use when fishing on bottoms covered with rocks since it doesn't get hung up as often as other types. The egg sinker is also good for rocky bottoms or coral reefs. It has a hole running through the center and slides up and down the line. To keep it away from the hook you tie on a barrel swivel, between line and leader, to act as a stop. You can also use pyramid sinkers for bottom fishing over sandy bottoms; they are specially popular in surf fishing.

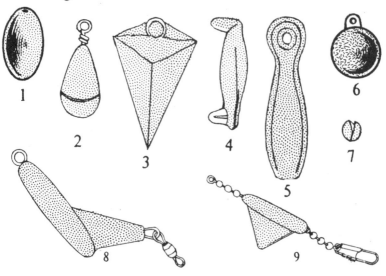

Displayed in the above art are some of the sinkers which are used for fishing on the bottom: 1. The Egg sinker, 2. Dipsey, 3. Pyramid (sand sinker), 4. Clinch, 5. Bank, 6. Ball, 7. Split-shot or Buckshot.

These two sinkers are used exclusively for trolling: 8. The Drail, and 9. The Keel. Each is designed to offer the angler the least amount of water resistance.

BOTTOM RIGS

Basic bottom rig has one hook on a short leader tied to a three-way or crossline swivel on the line. This hook can be tied just above the sinker or a foot or more above it, depending on the fish you are seeking. A variation of the one-hook rig is the two hook bottom rig. Here you tie the first hook near the sinker, and a second hook high enough to clear the first (as illustrated). You can also make a four or five-hook rig.

POPULAR BOTTOM FISHING RIGS

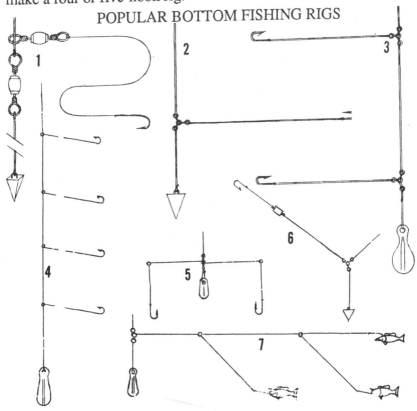

1. Single hook rig with sliding pyramid sinker (fish finder rig), 2. Single hook rig with pyramid sinker, 3. A two hook rig for baiting bottom and above bottom feeding fish, bank sinker, 4. A 4 hook rig usually used for mackerel for which the rig is named, 5. The Spreader rig often used for flounder fishing, 6. Floater, one hook rig, often used with a small block of cork on the hook leader or snell to lift the bait above the bottom, ideal for live and dead bait, 7. The dropper bait rig that has two or more hooks tied into the main hook leader or snell, dropper fashion, use live or dead small bait fish.

NATURAL BAITS

Bottom fishing anglers usually use natural baits, which can be purchased at tackle and bait stores, marinas, and fish markets, or you may want to catch your own. Seaworms such as clamworms, sandworms, pileworms, and bloodworms can be used to catch a great variety of fish. So are various kinds of clams found along the Atlantic and Gulf coasts. Strips of squid catch many bottom fish, as do crabs of many descriptions. Shrimp, both live and dead are excellent for many species. And baitfish such as pinfish, sand eels, killifish, pilchards, and mullet are also good when dead or alive. Larger fish can be cut up into chunks, steaks, or strips for bait. Along the Atlantic and the Gulf coasts bottom fishing is often done by "party boats," also called drift boats. They sail from most of the large cities and towns along the Atlantic and Gulf Coasts and charge for a half or a full day of fishing. More often than not rods, reels and baits are furnished. On the east coast anglers catch sea bass, porgies, flounders, flukes mackerels, bluefish and cod. On the Gulf Coast they catch many species of snappers and groupers,

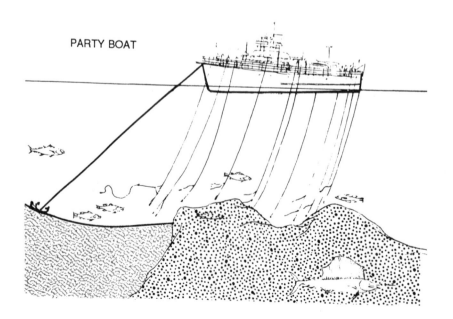

PARTY BOAT

HOOKING SALT WATER NATURAL BAITS

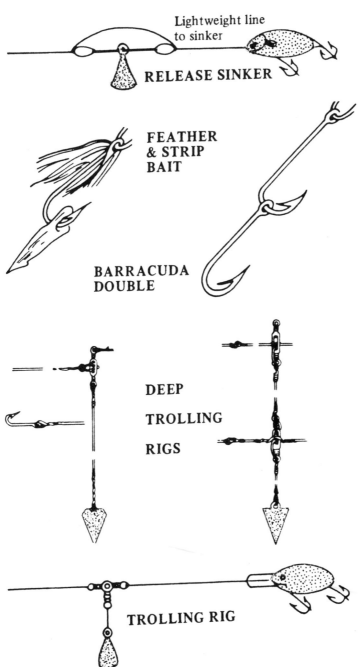

Lightweight line
to sinker

RELEASE SINKER

**FEATHER
& STRIP
BAIT**

**BARRACUDA
DOUBLE**

DEEP

TROLLING

RIGS

TROLLING RIG

HOOKING SALT WATER NATURAL BAITS

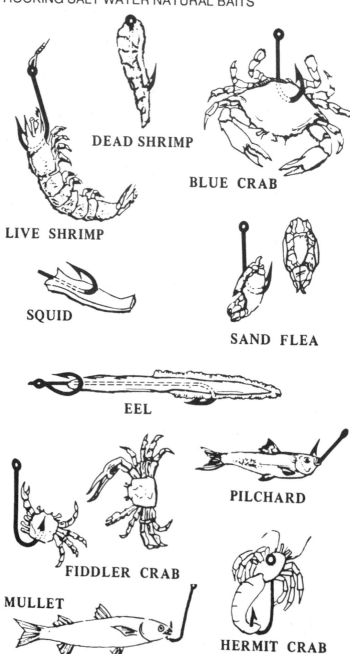

DEAD SHRIMP

BLUE CRAB

LIVE SHRIMP

SQUID

SAND FLEA

EEL

PILCHARD

FIDDLER CRAB

MULLET

HERMIT CRAB

A. Whole fish rigged for trolling or drift fishing. (Remove backbone for better trolling action). Hook may be added in the anal cavity area.

B. Headless fish rigged for drift or bottom fishing. (Hook may be added in the tail section).

C. How to hook a blue crab.

D. How to cut fish for "cut-bait"; for bottom fishing. (Entrails and tail can be ground up for chumming).

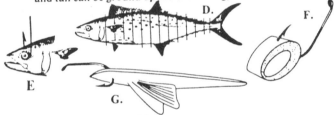

E. How to hook head of fish.

F. How to hook cut-bait.

G. Ventral or pelvic strip-bait for casting or trolling. (Pelvic strip area - dotted line).

H. Squid hooked for trolling or drift fishing.

I. How to hook squid head for bottom fishing. (Treble hook may be used by pushing hook shank and eye up through the mouth area in center of tentacles).

J. Eel rigged for casting or trolling. (Hook may be added in anal cavity area).

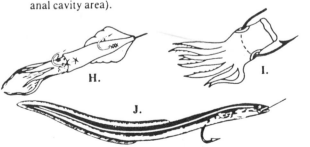

WHERE TO BOTTOM FISH

The angler must first remember that bottom feeding fish only congregate in areas where they can find food, shelter, and water temperatures to their liking. Bottom fishing can be done almost anywhere from which the angler can lower or cast a bottom fishing rig; pier, bank, surf, bridge, jetty, rocky shore or from a boat anchored close to the shoreline or any offshore waters, deep or shallow.

One of the most popular areas for bottom fishing is a broken or rocky bottom where sea worms, and crustaceans of many descriptions are available as well as many kinds of bait fish. Rocky bottoms are usually a hang-out for snappers, porgies, sea bass, amberjacks, and groupers. There are also many so called "banks" found in saltwater, these are in the form of submerged plateaus or shoals.

Shellfish beds of mussel, oysters and clams are also good places for bottom fishing, as are artificial and natural reefs. The latter may be either in deep or shallow water, but those that are exposed during a low tide should be fished throughout and one hour after the incoming high tide.

Breakwaters and jetties also offer good feeding grounds for bottom feeders. Rocks of jetties are often covered with many forms of crustaceans which are favored by sheepshead, redfish, black drum, etc. Always lay your baited rig along side the rocks or if at all possible lower it into a large hole between the rocks.

The pilings (wood or concrete) which support bridges, docks and piers are usually covered with oysters, barnacles and other molluscs and crustaceans. Dropping your baited rig off of these structures will often reward you with porgies, grunts, snappers, sheepshead and an occasional cobia or snook.

Offshore, in deeper water, can be found some of the best bottom fishing grounds, especially over submerged wrecks, rocky bottoms, reefs, and seaweeds. Reefs, and rocky bottoms are where many of the bottom feeders find food and plenty of shelter. A baited rig dropped among these fish attractors will usually result in an immediate strike from barracuda or an excellent tasting yellowtail snapper or grouper.

HOW TO LOCATE BOTTOM FISHING GROUNDS - A proven method of locating an ideal bottom fishing area is to drift your boat with a baited rig bouncing along the bottom. When you get a bite or a fish, keep drifting over the area or lower the anchor and fish the spot.

A good bet for attracting fish close to your baited rig is to fill a mesh-bag with ground, cut-up or chopped fish, or other sea animals (crabs, clams, oysters, squid, etc.) "chum". If no cloth mesh bag is available make a small chum cage using wire mesh fence material, but make sure that the mesh is not too large to allow ground or chopped chum to drift out of it. Whatever your choice be sure to lift it up and down off the bottom occasionally to allow the seafood oil to escape.

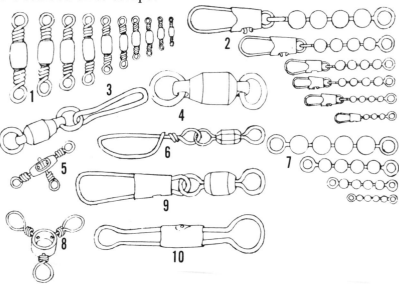

Above are some examples of the important pieces of equipment now being used by both the fresh and salt water anglers. 1. Assorted barrel swivels, 2. Bead chain snaps, 3. Link snap swivel, 4. Big game ball bearing, 5. 3-way barrel swivel, 6. Coastlock snap, 7. Bead chain swivels, 8. 3-way ring swivel, 9. Common snap w/swivel, 10. Connector.

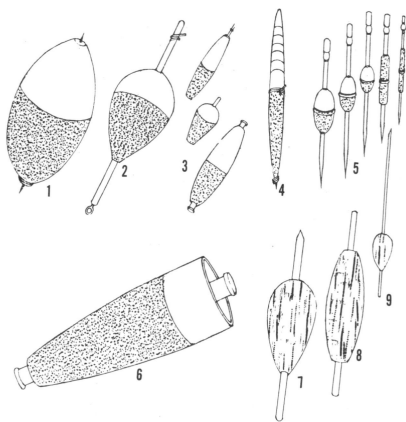

Floats commonly used by fresh and salt water anglers. 1. Casting, 2. Egg (bicolor), 3. Perch (3 kinds), 4. Hollow quill, 5. Panfish (5 kinds), 6. Popping, 7. Egg (natural), 8. Barrel (natural), 9. Stick-up.

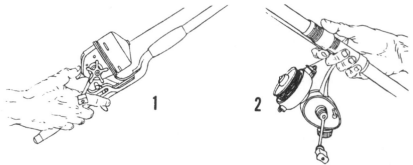

Two popular spinning reels; 1. Closed-face pushbutton type, 2. the open-face type. Both types are used equally as well for bait-casting and bottom fishing.

SALTWATER FISH AND HOW TO FISH THEM

There are literally thousands of fish species in our oceans. Used to great unobstructed spaces, many of them range widely and certain ones are migratory, appearing along each portion of our coasts only at certain times of the year. As in freshwater, most of the species serve as forage for the fewer large species.

It would be almost impossible to cover all saltwater species in a book of this size. However, since certain unusual or rare or unpopular species bite now and then when fishing is directed at specific game or food fish, methods given in the following pages successfully cover the entire field. Only those species most popular with anglers are described.

Very loosely, the more popular saltwater species may be put into the following classes: Big-Game Fish, General Game Fish; bottom fish. These groups greatly overlap, and even more than in freshwater angling, methods greatly overlap also. Commonly numerous species are caught while the angler is directing his endeavors toward a special favorite.

BIG GAME FISH: There are many species of fish that are recognized among salt water anglers and the International Game Fish Association (I.G.F.A.) as being big game fish. Some are extremely large while others are much smaller but are real fighters on rod and reel. These large game fish inhabit the open oceans and for one to pursue them successfully, one must invest a considerable amount of money in tackle and guide service, but for those who care to test themselves in battle against some of the most powerful of hook-and-line fishes, they are in for the thrill of a lifetime.

These large game fish are, in no way of great abundance species-wise, but a few of them with which the sport angler does battle with are the best of what the world's marine heavyweight class has to offer.

Getting back to the initial cash layout for owning your own big game tackle: For the newcomer who may want to try open water fishing can go another way to find out if he or she is qualified to take on the big test before investing in the purchase of their own saltwater tackle. The suggestion that follows is also directed to those who may only have the time for short and uncertain periods in salt water, may find it enjoyable and a learning experience to charter a boat, many of whom supply all of the big game fishing tackle needed, and a group of fine teachers of the trade, your skipper and crew. If the cost of the charter seems to be more than you care to spend, join a party of already booked anglers and just pay your share or get a group of your own from your list of angling friends, neighbors or the guys or gals from your office. However, there are many popular sport-fishing ports that have at least one large boat in operation which makes daily trips to offshore or bay fishing grounds on a come one come all basis. This is also a good way to get the opportunity to pay less, meet a lot of experienced anglers, however, here again, the skipper and crew is at your disposal for rigging tackle (supplied) and baiting up for you. Bait, of course, is always furnished by charter boats.

In many ports, boats are available which can be boarded at night. On these you rent a bunk and sleep while the boat runs out to the fishing grounds. A steward wakes you; you are served breakfast and other meals aboard; tackle is available at a cost that is seldom prohibitive for the average angler. Some of these boats furnish both trolling and bottom fishing tackle, and anglers fish with a rotation system so each angler gets a chance at the best, or stern, position. In some ports, offshore anchored barges are available. A speedboat taxi service runs you to the barge and planned return trips are made at regular intervals. On the barge, food and tackle can be purchased, use your own rod or rent one. My advice, to the new saltwater angler, if you plan on buying your own tackle (rod, reel, and the works), I suggest that you buy a surf outfit which can be easily used along the beach, or from a bridge, pier, jetty or boat. The cost, whatever it may be, will be well worth it.

FISH IDENTIFICATION

For proper identification of a fish it is necessary for the angler to learn the superficial structure of a fish. Coloration as positive identification can only be taken lightly. Individuals of the same species taken from different kinds of environment will show color changes. A good example is the snapper family, in particular, the dog snapper may have a background color of silver-gray or copper or brown, blended with red. Some specimens may be barred, others not. Also, all fish, after being caught and removed from the water wil show a rapid color change. A king white fish when first caught will have a dark greenish dorsal area, with silver-white sides and belly, but just 5 minutes on a stringer it begins to darken all over, and by the time of death it atains an all over darkness that would make it impossible to identify by color alone.

Therefore, taking all methods of identification into consideration, my personal feeling is that the outline of a specimen is the only method of positive identification of the species. All outlines of the artwork of fish throughout the book are accurate enought to enable the angler to compare and identify a catch properly. For further identification a count of fin spines of the first and second dorsal fin will further the accuracy. For instance, the common jack, blue runner, and the pompano are very often mistaken for one another, especially when mixed schools of these fish are feeding together. However, if the angler will examine the spinous dorsal fin (1st fin), separation is quite easy (see illustration

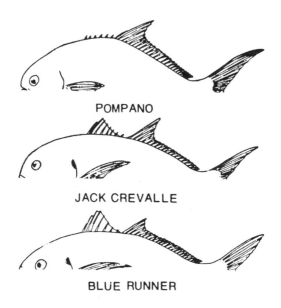

POMPANO

JACK CREVALLE

BLUE RUNNER

NAMES OF FISHES

Some species of fishes may have as many as five dozen common or angler's pet names. The names used in this book are the common names of the species that were selected in total agreement by the American Fisheries, the International Game Fish Association and the Outdoor Writers Association of America.

EXTERNAL ANATOMY OF A BONY FISH

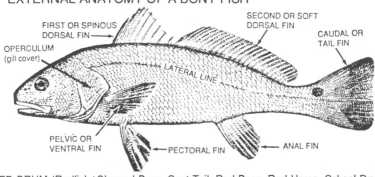

RED DRUM (Redfish, Channel Bass, Spot Tail, Red Bass, Red Horse, School Drum, Puppy Drum, etc.)

BIG-GAME FISHES

Big game fish of the heavyweight class are herein described, as are their habits, habitats, their natural foods, and the most popular ways to fish for them. Stout heart and tackle, and a little luck is all that is required by the saltwater angler.

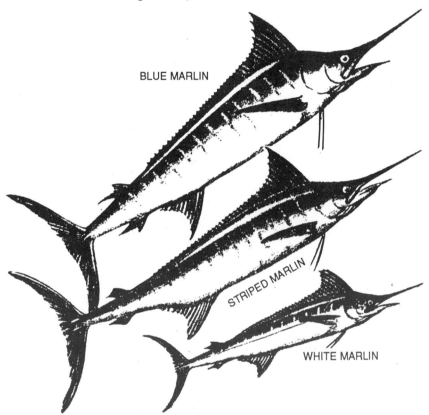

MARLINS, SAILFISHES AND SWORDFISHES are, collectively, referred to as "billfish." However, marlins and sailfish belong to the same family, but a swordfish is in a family by itself. The long extensions of their bill, or snouts are round in marlins and sail fish and flattened like the blade of a sword in the swordfish. Large swordfish have been known to ram a boat. In one particular incident, a swordfish drove its sword through planks that measured four inches thick. When hooked, they all will surge from the sea in leap after leap, shaking violently as they try to free themselves from the hook. An angler's fight with a sailfish may last for as much as an hour while the battle with a large marlin may last upwards to two hours, or more, but a large swordfish is capable of keeping the most experienced angler busy for as much as a half of a day or more, depending of course, on the weight of the swordfish. The weight of a large swordfish can tip the scales at 1,000 pounds or more, during a fight all of these fish alternately jump and bore deep into the water.

COMPARISON OF BILLS AND DORSAL FINS AMONG THE SWORD, SAILS, AND MARLINS.

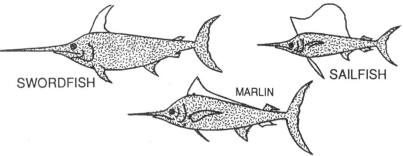

SWORDFISH

MARLIN

SAILFISH

One method of distinguishing these three fishes is by their dorsal fin. If the fin is high and about the same height as its full length, it is a sailfish. If the fin is highest in front, the fish is a marlin. And if the fin consists of a single tall lobe, it is a swordfish. Of the marlins, there are three separate species, the blue marlin, the striped marlin and the white marlin. White marlins live in the Gulf of Mexico and abundantly in the Atlantic as far north as Massachusetts. The white marlin is the smallest of the three, weighing up to 150 pounds. The blue marlin averages, in weight, 200 to 400 pounds, top weight is upwards to 2,000 pounds. It is found in the same territory but are more common in the caribbean farther south. Many also occur off the coast of Europe and Africa. Specimens weighing 2,000 pounds have been netted. One individual taken on rod and reel weighed 1,376 pounds. The swordfish is found worldwide in temperate and tropical oceans. This fish is also called broadbill or broadbill swordfish. It inhabits continental shelf waters from the surface to depths of 400 to 500 fathoms (a fathom is a unit of depth or length, equal to six feet). Spawning, however, takes place in cool, deep waters usually near sub-marine canyons or deep coral banks. The dorsal and pectoral fins of the swordfish are non-retractable, they are rigid; and a very large keel is present on each side of the caudal peduncle. Adult swordfish lack scales, and all sizes are without ventral fins. Coloration; the back may be dark brown, bronze, dark metallic purple, grayish blue or black. The sides may be dark like the back or dusky; the lower sides of the head and belly may be dirty white or brownish white.

Mentioned earlier was the attack by a swordfish which drove its bill through a four inch plank of a boat.

This brings to mind another incident where a swordfish attacked the *Woods Hole submersible, "Alvin," at a depth of 330 fathoms, and wedged its sword so tightly into a seam that it could not withdraw it.

* *Woods Hole Oceanographic Institution (WHOI)*
Woods Hole, Massachusetts

The natural foods of the swordfish include fish and squid. Fishing method most often used is trolling when swordfish are spotted close to the surface, or deep drift fishing especially during the night. In either method of fishing squid is most often the bait. However, all kinds of deep water fish (mackerels, dolphins (the fish), small tuna, bonito, the latter dead or alive, eel and mullet). For best results when fishing the surface is to clip your line to an outrigger which skitters the bait near or on the surface.

Swordfish often bask on the surface with their rigid dorsal fin protruding from the water. This habit makes them vulnerable to harpooners, who together with longliners (handline commercial fishingpersons) who together, account for most of the swordfish catches. Among many sport fishingpersons the swordfish is a coveted prize, difficult to locate, difficult to hook and difficult to compete with its tremendous fighting ability. The swordfish is also an important commercial species. Its light colored, firm flesh is with a unique flavor.

Swordfish are very finicky, and easily frightened by an approaching boat, and will rarely strike blindly. The bait must always be presented carefully, sometimes repeatedly before the big fish will take it, and there is always the risk, because of its soft mouth, that makes hooking uncertain, and of course, the long, slashing bill of the swordfish can make short work of the angler's line or leader.

When trolling for swordfish, upon sighting one, the speed of the boat should be slowed but not too drastically, and the bait should be eased quietly and gently in front of the fish. Once hooked solidly, the fight is on. It is said among big game fish anglers, to land a swordfish is the highest achievement in angling.

THE MARLINS: The three species of marlins are placed among the world's greatest game fish, spectacular leapers and vicious fighters. They very rarely take artificial lures, however, some success has been achieved when using large bucktails. Most marlins are fished from chartered boats, with guides, by trolling, using outriggers to skip or skitter the natural bait along the surface. Best baits include (whole) mullet, squid, dolphin (the fish), and bonito. Sometimes strip bait is used, as well as a whole flying fish or Spanish mackerel. The usual action that takes place during a strike is the marlins habit of hitting the bait with the bill, to kill it, then turning and grasping it in the mouth. Therefore, when trolling, this "bill tap" is felt first. The bait is then allowed quickly to stay in the area of the tap. This is done by releasing the brake on the reel. This allows the bait to drop back some distance on slack line so that the bait will appear dead or injured and hang suspended or gradually sink below the surface. As the marlin slowly circles, it will seize the bait, at this time the angler quickly puts on the reel brake and sets the hook hard, and the fight is on. However, should the angler miss, begin trolling immediately and try again.

Tackle for marlins must be heavy and the angler should wear a shoulder harness and a rod-butt holder. Rod should be of good quality as should the reel, a 10/0 to 16/0 will do: leader, about 25 feet long, No. 12 wire, cable type is usually preferred because marlins leaps are not likely to kink it.

The white marlin, the smallest of the three and the sailfishes that follow, average much smaller than the blue and striped species. However, they are included among the big game fishes because of their fighting ability.

The white marlin has a blue-green colored dorsal area; grayish vertical stripes; belly is silvery. It resembles a small blue marlin, and inhabits the Atlantic Ocean and the Gulf of Mexico in the offshore waters of Florida about March, farther north during summer. Sometimes travels in small schools. Average weight is about 100 pounds.

SAILFISH: There are two species of sailfish, the Atlantic sailfish and the Pacific sailfish. The Atlantic Species ranges from Florida and Texas to New York, and the Pacific species ranges throughout most of the Pacific coast to Monterey, California. Actually distribution is believed to be worldwide, however, there is still some doubt whether there is only one species of sailfish or several closely related species. One thing is for sure, those caught in the Pacific Ocean average out to be much larger than the Atlantic species.

Like the marlins, the sailfish is one of the fastest of all saltwater fishes, and speeds up to 60 knots (a unit of speed on one nautical mile an hour) have been quoted. However, conservative boat captains and crews consider that 20 to 30 knots may be more representative.

The sailfish is with a long, slender, vertically compressed body that tapers evenly towards the deeply forked tail The upper jaw is prolonged into a circular, needlelike bill. The main characteristic is its dorsal fin which is high and about the same height as its full length; Tail stalk or peduncle is with double keel; pelvic fins are long and retractable; there are two small anal fins and two free moving pectoral fins.

Coloration includes a dark blue or bluish purple dorsal area; flanks and belly are with yellowish gray hues, sometimes adorned with bluish gray vertical bars composed of blue patches or spots. When opened the sail is of a slaty or dark blue, with the membrane displaying a scattering of black spots. Average weight is about 65 pounds, but when including the Pacific species weights of 200 to 240 pounders have been caught. The function of the large sail-like sail-like dorsal fin is not yet clearly understood, however, it may serve them in maneuvering.

Althought sails are renowned as a sport fish, and capable of spectacular aerial acrobatics, they tire quickly. Many anglers enjoy the fight much better by using light saltwater tackle. Natural foods include flying fish, needlefish, anchovies, squid and octopus. Anglers will often troll large feathered jigs, bucktails and strip bait, or whole mullet, Spanish mackerel or bonito, squid, etc. Trolling with an outrigger is the best means of skipping or skittering the bait on the surface of the water. As in marlin and sword fishing, if a tap from the bill is felt, then the bait allowed to drop back without result of the second tap, the bait should be put in to action immediately. Sometimes the second tap occurs, thus making sure of a fish which would otherwise have been missed. Patience is a virtue! The usual action that takes place during a strike is like that of the marlins, it's their habit of hitting the bait with the bill to kill or stun it, then turn and grasp it in their mouth to swallow it. Therefore, when the first tap is felt; release reel brake and wait for the second tap or a hit and run, whatever it may be immediately put on the brake and simultaneously set the hook hard and deep.

Sailfish are usually caught in distant offshore waters. Most are caught along the Texas and Atlantic Coast of Florida and the Gulf of Mexico, largely in the warm waters of the Gulf Stream. The most productive months are from the first of the year to midsummer. Trolling from charter boats, with the same bait that is used for marlin, and handled in the same manner, is the way to go.

GAME FISH IN GENERAL: The game fish presented here is a group of fish that are considered by the average saltwater angler to be of top notch sport qualities, and though a few of them require the use of a charter boat and guides, many can be taken from small boats rather close inshore with inexpensive tackle. In fact, a great number of them can be caught from bridges, piers, jetties and surf. For the most part they are every "angler's fish," and some of the fastest and best fighters are among them. Most are of good table quality and the rest are ideal for sport, the latter, if no other use for them than the fight they give they should be released for others to enjoy. This is a group of fish with which the average angler who spends either a lot of time or an occasional period on salt water will be most concerned, and in which they will find a wide variety of sport to suit their every notion or whim.

For convenience to the reader these fish are not listed according to families. Instead they are listed alphabetically.

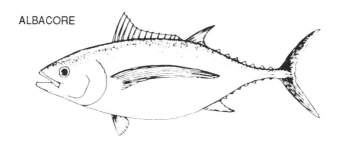

ALBACORE

ALBACORE: Atlantic and Gulf of Mexico off the Florida coast; uncommon farther north. In the Pacific it is abundant off the southern portion of California. The albacore is often mistaken for a small tuna, into which family it belongs. However, the characteristics that separates it from the true tunas are the pectoral fins, which on the albacore are extremely long, being almost half as long as the entire fish, and the albacore lacks the stripes and spots on the lower flanks that are present on the true tunas, and the albacore is with a white trailing edge on the margin of the tail fin, and lastly the albacore's deepest part of its body is near the second dorsal, rather than near the middle of the first dorsal fin as in true tunas.

Albacores are fast swimmers. Their dorsal fins fit into slots on their backs so that they create no friction when the fish is traveling at top speed. To give the angler an idea of movement and speed, an albacore tagged by biologists off the coast of California was caught two weeks later by commercial fishing persons near Japan. It was estimated to have traveled about 400 miles per day.

Millions of pounds of albacore are harvested every year off the western coast of the United States. Tremendously large schools appear in offshore waters in early summer and may still be present in the fall. Schools of smaller fish appear first, then the heavyweights. The white meat of the albacore is canned and sold as "Chicken of the Sea."

Fishing methods for albacore include trolling with feathered jigs, spoons; live bait such as mullet, sauries, herring, sardines, anchovies, and other small fishes as well as squid. Strips of mullet or Spanish mackerel are also good. Trolling at fast speeds is the key. When an albacore hits the bait set the hook hard and then be ready for action as it is a hard fighting fish that will take the bait deep down; when it stops running or diving begin "pumping" it up to the boat. Average weight about 15 pounds, maximum about 70 pounds.

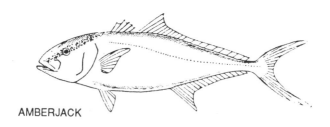

AMBERJACK

AMBERJACK: A fish that can be encountered in the Atlantic Ocean north to Carolinas, and along the western offshore waters off Florida in the Gulf of Mexico. This fish is a popular sport fish but many anglers do not eat them, however, their flesh when steamed is unequalled when used in a fish salad recipe. An amberjack is a large member of the jack family that may grow to the length of 5 or 6 feet and weigh upwards to 120 pounds or more. Amberjacks travel in schools in tropical waters throughout the world. It is a powerful fighting fish that is pale bluish silver with yellowish fins. A good field mark is the dark olive colored diagonal stripe that reaches from the mouth across the eye to about the first dorsal fin.

Troll around reefs, using strip bait, or feathered jigs, large spoons, etc. The amberjack is noted for its speedy runs into coral or other rocky places when hooked. Heavy tackle is the answer when pursuing this fish because it is very necessary to stop its powerful runs, otherwise you can easily lose your rig and fish. A 6/0 reel spooled with 300 yards of 60 pound test and a No. 8 wire leader with a No. 8 hook is adequate. When an angler catches the first amberjack, it is usually left on the hook and towed behind the boat because others in the school may follow this decoy and be hooked.

BARRACUDA

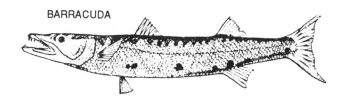

BARRACUDA: A fish that occurs in all tropical seas except the East Pacific. It is found around reefs, wrecks, piers, and sandy and grassy flats. Large specimens are usually loners, young are most often in schools. This fish should be regarded as a dangerous species because of its ability to inflict dangerous wounds upon a person, in or out of the water. Its bite is straight and clean.

Small barracuda supply anglers with great sport when hooked on light tackle, even the fly rod. However, large specimens may grow upwards to 90 pounds.

Coloration is bluish or dark on the dorsal area, silvery on sides and belly, with some indistinct dark spots. Natural foods consist mostly of fish of all descriptions plus just about anything else that crawls or swims in the oceans.

Fishing methods for catching this fearless fighter includes trolling when the big ones are desired, but for general barracuda fishing, bait casting or still fishing in any area around reefs, wrecks, both offshore, and in certain areas around inlets and other protected areas, including small, deep lagoons. At times, using lightweight bait casting tackle to cast spoons, and mullet strip-bait, bays and near-shore shoals will bring excellent results. A heavy saltwater fly rod using a large streamer, fished slowly is also very good for small and medium sized barracuda. In any type of fishing a heavy wire, single strand or braided is a must. As a food fish barracuda is very questionable. I have eaten very small individuals, 1 to 2 feet in length and enjoyed their flesh fried, but around the caribbean sea some people have died or got violently ill from eating barracuda. However, in California many restaurants include barracuda on their menus. Eating them is not really as important as catching them.

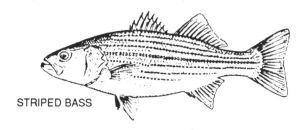

STRIPED BASS

BASS, STRIPED: Often called stripper or rockfish. This species is by far the most sought after surf fishing target of many anglers. The striped bass occurs from the St. Lawrence River to northern Florida on the Atlantic side, and in the Gulf of Mexico - Louisiana, Alabama and Mississippi, and along the U.S. Pacific coast from Washington to California. Although comparatively new (introduced) on the Pacific coast, on the east coast they have been well known to salt water anglers, and one of the most important food fishes since the early 1600's. The species moves far upstream in rivers during spawning migrations, and has a native range (in fresh water) from the St. Lawrence River, N.Y., south to St. Johns River, Florida. In some of these waters large populations have become landlocked due to artificial impoundments that blocked their return to the sea. In recent years the striped bass has been introduced into many freshwater lakes and rivers throughout

68

the nation. In fact the all-tackle record, 59 pounds 12 ounces was taken from the Colorado River in Arizona.

Striped bass is easily recognized by the 7 or 8 prominent black stripes that run along the sides of the fish's long, silvery body, one stripe running along the lateral line. It is a voracious and opportunistic predator that will consume all kinds of fish. The spawning period takes place in fresh or brackish waters during the latter part of April on through early June.

Fishing methods are varied. Saltwater fly rods are used as well as freshwater bait casting tackle, and of course heavy surf casting tackle. Many of these fish are taken by offshore trolling. Fly rod artificials include large and medium sized streamers and other dry flies, as well as popping bugs, like those used for largemouth bass. When bait casting, use any largemouth or large pike plugs, spoons and pork rind, and very deadly are large plastic worms and eels, and feathered jigs. Any of the aforementioned can be used in saltwater or inland freshwater systems. However, the best kind of fishing to get the full feel of the fight, surf fishing is best. Most types of fishing for strippers is best during the early evening on through the night and early morning hours. Trolling near shore, around river mouths and small bays using an eel skin rig, spoons, and spinners are equally effective during the day and night. Anyway you choose to fish be sure that it is done during an incoming tide which furnishes the best results.

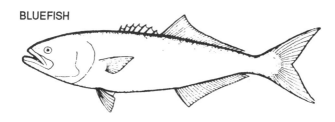

BLUEFISH

BLUEFISH: Also called the marine piranha, chopper, rock salmon, plus about a dozen more regional names. Florida, including the Gulf of Mexico, and along the eastern coastline in the

Atlantic. It is a streamlined, elongated, blue gray and silvery fish with a very deeply notched tail. The mouth is filled with extremely sharp teeth, and the second dorsal fin is with a very rigid sharp spine. It is a voracious fish which rightfully deserves the nicknames "marine piranha" and "chopper" because of its habit of swimming in schools along the beaches attacking swimmers and waders, and the feeding habit is nothing short of maniac, swimming through shoals of bait fish, slashing and destroying everything in its path, including smaller fish of its own kind. The bluefish's bite can cause a nasty wound on a human and the bite of a large individual can severe a finger or toe. As many careless anglers will attest, bluefish can be dangerous when out of the water. It is very active and hard to hold while a hook is being removed. It is said that some anglers are capable of sniffing out bluefish by their smell which is said to smell like cucumbers. Herpetologists also sniff out the venomous copperhead snake which is said to have the identical odor.

The methods of catching this battler which is so greedy that it will strike at practically any moving lure. Good natural baits include mullet, menhaden and squid. Artificials like bucktails, feathered jigs, spoons and spinners are also very effective. Many bluefish are caught in the surf using standard surf casting tackle. Inside waters, bays and mouths of brackish water inlets and outlets are excellent places to use sturdy bait and fly casting tackle. Surface and diving plugs, poppers and other largemouth bass and pike artificials are all good for the bluefish. Streamers, and other wet flies for the fly rod will account for some catches. For trolling, drift and still fishing - hook size should be from 3/0 to 6/0. When still fishing chumming with chopped Spanish mackerel, menhaden, the oilier the fish the better. The baited hook is then drifted or cast into the oily slick on the surface of the water which is caused by the oily-fish chum. Weights from 1 to 25 pounds are the averages. The flesh of the bluefish has the tendancy of becoming soft if not iced immediately and eaten as soon as possible. If time allows clean and fillet immediately after taking a blue from the water and decapitating it to allow bleeding. It is a flesh that will not keep for a long time, even when frozen.

BONEFISH: A fish that was once very common in the Florida Keys. Anglers at one time traveled from all parts of the world to test their skill against a bonefish. Occurs in shallow waters around flats and intertidal areas. It is a pale brownish fish with silvery sides and belly; parts of the snout and fins display a yellowish or dusky color. Structure is rather chunky, but very streamlined, with mouth set far under, and an odd, overlapping humped snout. Weights average 2 to 6 pounds maximum, about 15 pounds.

Bonefish are basically schooling fish. The smaller ones can often be observed in large schools on the flats. Larger individuals tend to form smaller schools or groups. The bonefish feeds on all kinds of small fish, crabs, shrimp, clams, sea worms, and sand fleas, etc. This fish is capable of giving any angler a lot of excitement when hooked on light or medium saltwater tackle.

All methods of fishing for bonefish around the Florida Keys should be done during the spring and summer months and early fall. Wariness of this fish and the shallow water make "bone-fishing" a real challenging sport. It can be done wading, or from a double-anchored skiff. Once the bonefish's feeding grounds have been located, the angler gets set, tackle ready to bring into play, as soon as the high tide begins to move in, waiting for swirling or "tailing" fish. Bonefish are often seen rooting in the sand for molluscs, their tails breaking the surface of the shallow water. This action is known as "tailing." At other times they will plough the bottom stirring up silt and marl. Such action is known as "mudding." Very often chum of shrimp, crab and clams is thrown out, the baited hook, with a very light sinker, or no sinker following. The bite of a bonefish is a slight tug as the fish mouths the bait,

BONEFISH

71

when the tug is felt the angler should set the hook immediately. Fly rod fishing with heavy tackle using size 1/0 trout flies can be a lot of fun. The fly is quietly cast very close to the feeding fish. Having plenty of backing line on a large single-action reel. Bonefish are awesomely swift, strong, never-say-die fighters. Bonefish are solely fished for sport and should be released. It is too bony to make good eating.

TUNAS: All are members of the mackerel family, and all are swift swimmers that travel in schools through warm temperate seas throughout the world. Among the tunas are some of the most famous game fish in the world. Some are important commercially.

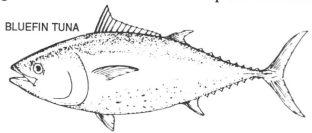

BLUEFIN TUNA

BLUEFIN TUNA: One of the largest fishes in the sea is also the most sought after tuna by sport anglers who want to test their angling skills against one of the most powerful fighters in the ocean wilderness. Tuna, when traveling will feed on small schooling fish that cross their path. Food include menhaden, Spanish mackerel, flying fish, etc. The schools of small tuna are called "school tuna" by anglers and average 20 to 100 pounds. Real large tuna, weighing from 200 to over 1000 pounds are called "horse mackerel."

Coloration include a dark blue dorsal area, flanks paling to grayish or silvery; belly and cheeks are silvery; dorsal fins dusky blue gray; dorsal and anal finlets tinged with yellow; pectoral fin short, tail is crescent shape. Size will usually vary according to distribution - up to 1,000 pounds in some areas while in some other areas specimens will measure up to 14 feet and weigh up to 1,800 pounds.

Bluefins range along both our coastlines, but the most famous fishing grounds are in the water off Bimini, West Indies, winter and spring; New Jersey to Nova Scotia, summer and fall. The best fishing method is trolling along offshore banks and at tide rips. Chumming is a very important part of tuna fishing - dropping overboard chunk herring and Spanish mackerel is the usual procedure, with the hook, baited with whole herring or Spanish mackerel, drifting with the chum each time it is thrown overboard. In some areas drift or still fishing and chumming brings excellent results.

When tuna are schooling close to the surface, trolling with an outrigger is very effective when natural baits are used. The skipping and skittering of natural bait resembles flying fishes, one of the main sources of food for all tunas.

Trolling for large tuna (horse mackerel) should only be done from a charter boat with an experienced captain/guide, and a good crew. Why? Well, when a large bluefin is hooked you are going to need all the help you can get. Playing a large tuna renowned for its tremendous strength requires a captain who knows how to manuever the boat to your advantage, and a crew member comes in handy to pour cold water over your hot reel, and to be ready to help should the fighting chair break loose from the deck.

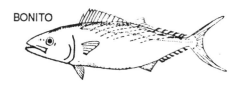
BONITO

BONITOS: Fish that are shaped very much like a tuna to which they are closely related. There are four species that swim in our waters and all are noted for their speed, power and fighting ability when hooked. Coloration includes blue on the upper parts; silvery and yellowish below. All have dark stripes running the length of their body, but on a slight upward angle; head is large and body is torpedo-shaped. All four species are schooling fish. The striped bonito usually lives in large shoals, in the open surface waters well off of the Atlantic and Gulf of Mexico shorelines of Florida, Texas, Alabama, Mississippi, Georgia and the Carolinas, and on to Massachusetts. The striped species averages between 15 and 20 pounds.

Most catches of bonito are accidentals for the fact that they are usually caught while fishing for other surface feeding fishes. It is for this reason that the angler use medium to heavy trolling tackle because there is a good chance of tying into something bigger than you're fishing for. Strip natural baits are good. Artificials; feathered jigs and spoons are sometimes very rewarding. The flesh of the bonitos are considered not very tasty.

KING MACKEREL

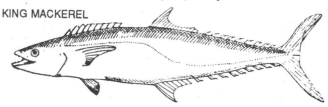

CERO, OR KING MACKEREL: This fish is easily distinguished from the bonitos by its high dorsal fin, slender form and spotted sides; and from small tunas by color, and dorsal fins. Coloration includes a dark blue on the upper half of the first dorsal fin. Dorsal area is deep blue shading to silver on the the sides and belly, and rows of oval-shaped yellowish orange spots on sides. A very popular small game fish that will bring anglers out by the hundreds when the king is running. Small examples are often used as bait for larger game fishes. Excellent as a table fish. Heavy commercializing on the species has depleted the population to such an extent that seasons open and close when you least expect it. This is true on both coastlines of Florida. Always check with the local bait shops for laws concerning the king mackerel seasons.

RED DRUM: Also called channel bass, redfish, spot-tail bass, red bass, plus many other regional names. This fish is found along the Atlantic coast from New Jersey to Florida and also along the coasts of the Gulf of Mexico. Coloration includes an overall coppery tinge, the nose is blunt and the tail fin square across the tip;

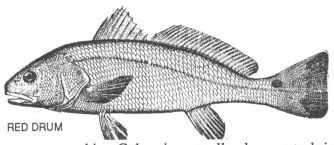

RED DRUM

belly a coppery white. Coloration usually changes to brick red after death. This fish can be easily recognized by its most outstanding characteristic which is a black spot on each side of the tail, about the size of the fish's eyes. Sometimes there are two spots, sometimes more, some may even appear on the body.

The red drum is a schooling fish that occurs inshore over mud or sandy bottoms. It inhabits both salt and brackish water and occasionally will live in freshwater lakes and rivers. When small, the fish will feed in rivers, sounds, and inlets, larger specimens feed in the surf and around pier and bridge pilings. The average weight is about 5 pounds, but fish weighing 10 pounds are not uncommon. The smaller ones up to 15 pounds are called "puppy drum." The rod and reel record is 90 pounds. It is a strong, hard fighter when hooked.

Fishing method for large individuals is surf casting. For the average size fish, piers, bridges, and bays are best. Both large and small specimens may be caught while drifting, still-fishing and slow trolling almost anywhere close to the shorelines wherever the red drum lives. In the shallow, sandy and grassy flats this drum may be fished "bonefish style." Natural baits include crabs, shrimp, clams, sea worms, finger mullet, and sand bugs or fleas. Artificials can be weighted bucktails, feathered jugs, and streamer flies for the fly-rodder. Upwards to 15 pounds red drum is good eating. Larger specimens may be a little coarse for some people.

COBIA: Also called crab-eater. A fish of Florida and Carolina waters. It is a long dark brown to cream colored fish, solid as a mackerel, and a powerful fighter that is considered a prize when caught and a prize for the table. Its flesh is absolutely delicious, baked, broiled or fried.

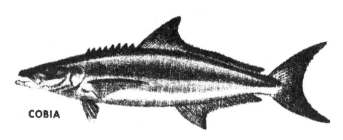

COBIA

The cobia has a striking resemblance to the remora (shark sucker) but lacks the sucking discs on the top of the head. The average weight of a cobia is less than 10 pounds, but a rod and reel record weighed 135 pounds and measured more than 5 feet in length.

As a game fish, the cobia is highly rated as a hard hitting fish with a lot of fighting spirit, and are prone to long, powerful, determined runs and a leap or two, here and there. They are not an easy fish to bring to the gaff, just about half of them hooked are lost. Although large individuals are solitary fish, the small ones usually travel in small schools and when one is hooked, at least another individual can be observed swimming with it. Sometimes the entire group or school will surface with it. It is a fish that hangs around boat markers and buoys as well as the pilings of piers and bridges.

Methods of fishing include trolling with natural or artificial baits. Bottom fishing, drift fishing, and surf casting. Its favorite foods include many forms of crustaceans, especially crabs of all kinds.This habit has given it the nickname "crab eater." It is not a common fish anywhere and most are caught by accident, for instance, many are hooked by anglers fishing for spotted trout (weakfish) in the weedy flats, and also by anglers fishing for black drum around piers and bridges. The latter of course is a devout crab eater too. Ideal baits also include small fish, squid, stripped,or whole mullet and shrimp.

DOLPHIN: The fish, not the sea mammal of "Flipper" fame. This is one of the most beautifully colored of all gamefishes. The dolphin is so distinctive in body shape and color that it cannot be mistaken for any other fish. The male, or bull, has a high, straight

76

forehead; the head of the female is also high but has a distinct upward slope to the dorsal fin. Coloration includes a dorsal fin. A mid dorsal area of deep ocean blue, grading into green on the upper sides and yellow from the lateral line to the silver belly. The sides are sprinkled with a mixture of light and dark spots. The dorsal fin starts far forward, almost directly over the eyes, and extends back to the deeply forked tail; the anal fin is also long, stretching over about half the length of the body. The laterally compressed body is streamlined, tapering sharply from head to tail The dolphin is one of the fastest swimmers, dashes upwards to 50 miles per hour have been authenticated. As many anglers will attest, the run of a hooked dolphin will make your line sing as it is stripped from the reel. This fish ranges from the Gulf of Mexico to the Carolinas; California to Oregon. It is an open ocean fish that feeds on all kinds of smaller fish, however, it seems to be extremely fond of flying fish. May be a loner or in small schools. Weight averages about 5 pounds with 20 pounders not being uncommon, many have been caught weighing as much as 50 pounds. The record is somewhere around 85 pounds.

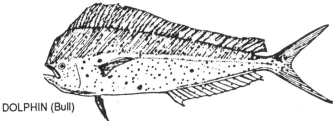

DOLPHIN (Bull)

Methods of fishing include trolling with strip bait, (preferably from an outrigger), whole mullet or flying fish or metal spoons or feathered jigs. Light tackle for sport or heavy tackle if you want to make sure that you bring some home for dinner. The trick of successful school-dolphin fishing is to tire the first one hooked, then keep it in the water, close to the boat without landing it. This method will usually hold the school together, and often others will be close enough for bait casting. Active anglers using this method have been known to clean out a school in short order. When hooked, a dolphin will often leap or tailwalk, darting first in one direction and then another. Runs are extremely fast and powerful, high-test lines have been snapped by fish half the weight of the line-test. This usually happens when the brake is prematurely engaged or the drag being changed while the fish is running, the latter action have cost many anglers many good fish, especially on a reel that is equipped with a star drag.

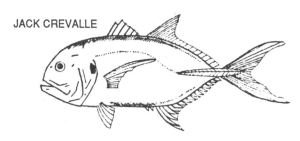
JACK CREVALLE

JACKS: There are several species of fish that are named "Jacks." All are members of a family of fish that includes the pompanos.
table fish while the pompana is held in high esteem as a table fish. Jacks are found in both Atlantic and Pacific, with the latter area being less common. Most common in the Gulf around Florida, the jack or jack crevalle. A fish with a steep, blunt forehead, deep body, forked tail, and a lateral line that is deeply curved down toward the tail, and with bony plates along the caudal peduncle. Coloration includes an irridescent gray-blue and yellowish body. All jacks in general are swift, stubborn battlers and are considered standard sport fish that will hit almost any artificial or natural bait. Offshore whoppers are usually taken while trolling for other fish when strip bait, spoons, feather jigs and the like are used. Surf fishing will sometimes offer a large individual, but all around good jack fishing is bait casting in bays, inlets, channels, either from the shoreline or from a boat. Yellow feathers and plugs usually prove to be the best color. As mentioned earlier, jacks are not especially good for the table, however, this writer has prepared them by cutting out the liver line of fillets and found the white flesh to be very tasty any way cooked. Steamed flesh is hard to beat for salads and gumbos.

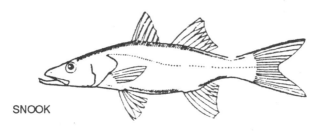

SNOOK

SNOOK: A large fish with a big mouth, two dorsal fins, and a narrow dark stripe down the side. Body is robust, slightly compressed; head depressed; lower jaw projecting beyond upper; cheeks scaly. Coloration includes dark olive to bluish above, whitish below; a conspicuous narrow black stripe along the lateral line. Attains a weight up to 50 pounds or more.

The snook is in abundance around Florida and the Gulf of Mexico coastline. Feeds on all kinds of small fish and shrimp. Brackish water rivers, inlets, mud flats, mangrove shorelines, sandy channels and even fresh water lakes and rivers that link to the fish's saltwater habitat are the places to fish for them. The snook is a bait casters delight that will smash almost any artificial, surface, divers, or sinking kinds. Fly rodders will do well with large wet flies and streamers. Best fishing is at night around bridges, piers and the surf or still-fishing, with a lantern, a little offshore. In elusiveness the snook is often compared with the northern freshwater fish, the muskelunge. Many anglers go forth in quest of these two fish, but very few catch a musky or snook.

Anglers landing a snook should be extremely careful during the process of removing the hook, the gill cover is serrated and as sharp as a razor. The snook is an excellent table fish with delicate, white, flaky meat.

TARPON: A proportionately large fish with large, silvery scales, a deeply forked tail, large mouth, and with the last ray of the dorsal fin greatly elongated. Body is compressed; the lower jaw juts out and up. Coloration; bluish silvery above, silvery on sides and underparts. The tarpon is most abundant about Florida's Atlantic coastlines and the coastlines of the Gulf of Mexico. Food

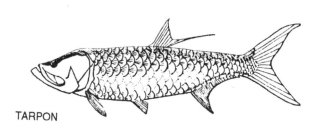

TARPON

includes all kinds of small fish, crabs and shrimp.

The tarpon is one of our greatest game fish, a desperate fighter and a spectacular leaper. Its bony mouth makes it hard to set a hook, and when hooked, leaps make it almost impossible to keep it hooked. Tarpon anglers usually comb the surface of the water for schools of rolling and feeding fish. When sighted anglers will try trolling slowly, with natural baits, usually strip bait; artificials and spoons. Many anglers prefer to still fish with a live or dead mullet. The latter, when left lying on the bottom often proves successful as are whole blue crabs. Bobber fishing with pinfish and large jumbo shrimp is also effective. Hook sizes should be 9/0 to 11/0, leader No. 9 about 6 feet in length. Plug casting and popping bugs when fishing for small tarpon in bayous and canals is very sporty

also. When fly fishing for this fish, nothing short of heavy equipment should be used with plenty of line backing for the initial run and the up and coming leaps. Tarpon is not a table fish and should be released back into the water.

WAHOO

WAHOO: This fish is found worldwide in tropical and warm temperate seas, and are somewhat abundant in our waters off the Florida coastlines, mostly off the southern part of the peninsula and the keys. It is a loner or swims about in small groups. There is no special way of fishing exclusively for wahoo for most catches are accidentally hooked while fishing for other game fish. Coloration is blue or green above, silvery below. It is a fish with great speed and great fighting ability. It is a powerful fish with a heavily toothed mouth. It is solitary in deep waters of the open sea and along deep offshore reefs. Average weight is about 15 pounds; maximum over 100 pounds. Method is trolling with strip bait, or spoons, and feathered jigs. Wahoos are usually caught while trolling for dolphin, marlins, or sailfish. Wire leader is very essential.

WEAKFISHES: Weak fishes or sea trouts include about 15 different species. They are found along the Atlantic and Pacific coasts of North America. All are slim-bodied and trout-like in appearance. The name weakfish applies to the tender mouths from which hooks tear easily. Many anglers use landing nets when fishing from the shoreline or boat to keep from losing their catch. The common weakfish and the speckled species are rather common in the surrounding waters of Florida. The speckled species is very popular among sport anglers as well as recreational anglers and are caught by bait casting or still fishing while wading, from the shoreline or from a boat. Shrimp is about the best bait, artificials include all kinds of jigs. The grass flats are the best places to fish for them, although many are caught from piers and bridges. In an emergency this writer used a weighted hook and a strip of white cloth torn from a handkerchief, with much success.

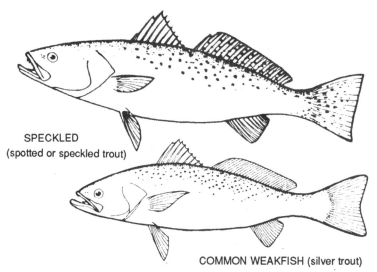

SPECKLED
(spotted or speckled trout)

COMMON WEAKFISH (silver trout)

Both species are olive to grayish above and with spots, however, the common species is with small spots on the sides while the speckled is with larger black spots that not only are scattered about the body, but also the dorsal fins as well as the tail fin. All weakfish are considered fine table fish.

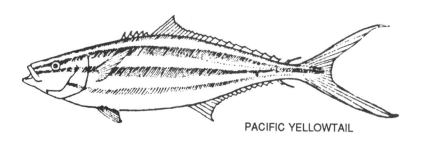

PACIFIC YELLOWTAIL

PACIFIC YELLOWTAIL: Often call "amberjack", and it is shaped like its Florida relative the Greater Amberjack. However, the Florida Yellowtail is not related, but is a member of the Snapper family. In the Pacific species, the colors are separated by a light lemon yellow stripe running along the median line from tail to eye.

The yellowtail is a coastal schooling fish that stays close inshore, around rocks, feeding on small school fish. It is one of California's top game fish. Can be taken surf casting at proper locations, but it is most often fished by trolling herring or sardines, or metal spoons and feathered jigs. Weight averages about 10 to 15 pounds; maximum about 75 pounds. The yellowtail is a fast swimmer and its strike is vicious, however, when the fish hits the bait allow slack in the line and time for the fish to swallow the bait before setting the hook hard.

BOTTOM FISH

Among the following described fishes are no game fish, and they hardly qualify as sport fishes, however, all are very much fished for by recreational anglers and all are fun to catch and fine to eat. Many are caught while fishing in the surf for game fish, while many are taken by still-fishing anglers from the shoreline or a boat. Methods of fishing seldom differ for any particular species. Only the most popular and most important bottom fish are presented.

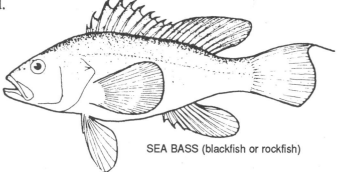

SEA BASS (blackfish or rockfish)

SEA BASS: Aslo called blackfish and rockfish, This is one of the most commonly caught by anglers while bottom fishing for groupers. Its range includes the western North Atlantic ocean along the United States east coast from Massachusetts to the Gulf of Mexico. The black sea bass is, as a rule, a deep water species that inhabits rocky bottoms and offshore reefs, however, many are caught by anglers fishing from piers with deep drop-offs, or by those that fish around wrecks, and over shell beds. This fish can be caught throughout the year, however, from May to June and from

November to December are the best times to fish for them. When hooked on light to medium saltwater tackle, the sea bass will fight all the way up to the surface. The fight presented by this fish, according to many anglers rate it very much a game fish. Coloration: grayish to black, with indistinct mottlings or stripes. Natural foods include crabs, clams, small fish, etc. These also prove out to be the best bait, but many are also taken on fish chunks.

As a food fish the flesh of the black sea bass is delicate in flavor, it is white and firm.

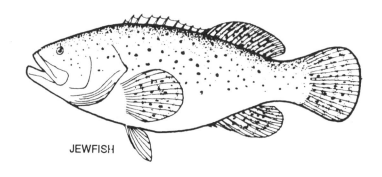

JEWFISH

JEWFISH: There are two species, the species in the Pacific Ocean is called the California sea bass and the other around Florida is called the spotted jewfish. It is a large fish with a huge mouth and a body that is dark and mottled with a lighter color than that of the background color. Rocky bottoms near jetties in deep waters, around wharves, and in inlets and channels are the places to fish for it, all are places where it feeds mainly on crustaceans, etc., also includes fish in its diet. It has been known to inhale an occasional sea turtle into its enormous mouth. The jewfish is the largest member of the grouper family, attaining lengths upwards to 8 feet and weights exceeding 700 pounds. The large specimens often live in underwater caves, and are very sluggish and very protective of their domain, and are very curious and have been known to approach scuba divers. Some have even attempted to swallow a diver, and there are some authenticated records where a huge fish had held divers by the arm, leg or head, in their large mouth, and caused their death by drowning.

Large jewfish offer the angler very little fight, but its great size and weight are hard to handle, especially from depths of more than 200 feet. However, the only defense a jewfish has against an angler is its habit of swimming into a hole or betwen rocks when it is hooked, making it difficult for the mightiest of anglers with heavy equipment to bring the jewfish to the surface to land it. Small jewfish, under a 100 pounds are much more active when hooked and will resist the angler from the bottom of the sea all the way up to the surface. They are fun to catch and the small ones are fine to eat. However, the large ones are very fine to eat, but how does one fillet a 500 pound jewfish?

Methods for fishing is usually started with a very large hook, sometimes a rope for a line, whole fish of several pounds or a few crabs (large blue crabs are good), fished on bottom, either still or from a drifting boat. Smaller jewfish will occassionally hit on slowly trolled, deep running spoons and feathered jugs. As mentioned earlier the jewfish regardless of size are good eating, but, fishing for it can be more labor than sport.

GROUPERS: There are many species of grouper in both the Atlantic and Pacific oceans, but in the Atlantic range they are most abundant around the offshore waters of Florida coastline and the Gulf of Mexico coastline, they have a tendency to thin out north of the Carolinas. The shape of groupers are very similar to that of the largemouth bass of freshwater fame. Species: black, red, yellow, Nassau, rock groupers, red hind, tripletail, etc. All species are spotted or mottled, usually somberly, natural foods include small fish, crabs, and shrimp. Average weight, 5 to 25 pounds, maximum, over 100 pounds.

Groupers are very popular among charter boats that go to grouper grounds far offshore in depths of 100 feet or more. Offshore trolling with strips of mullet attached to a spoon, or by

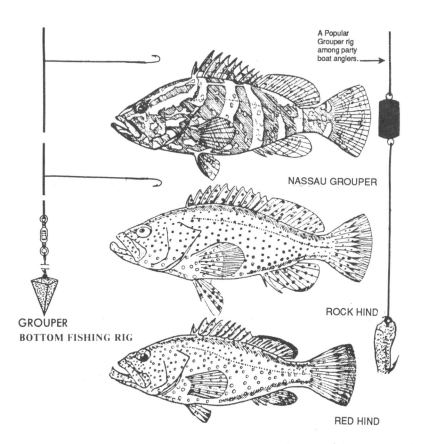

A Popular Grouper rig among party boat anglers. →

NASSAU GROUPER

ROCK HIND

GROUPER
BOTTOM FISHING RIG

RED HIND

still-fishing over deep rocky reefs. They can be fished in bays and inlets, trolling with feather jigs, spoons, and plugs, or by still-fishing close to the bottom with chunk (cut) bait, and shrimp. Rod should be of medium weight, line at least 40 pound test and the hook about 8/0 for groupers can run heavy, and fight hard and deep, and must often be turned before they get a chance to run in rocks or other shelters. Groupers change colors quickly when taken from the water. All are excellent eating fish.

SNAPPERS: More than 250 species make up this important family of fish found in the warm seas throughout the world. Some are fished commercially, others are considered sport fishes. Snapper are distinguished from the groupers by having pointed pectoral fins. The midwest range of snappers includes the Atlantic and Gulf coast, with the red snapper being the most sought after by commercial fisheries and sport anglers. This large snapper inhabits water

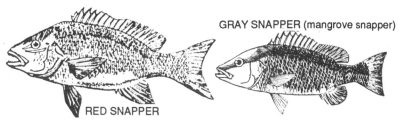

GRAY SNAPPER (mangrove snapper)

RED SNAPPER

150 feet or deeper. Many are caught by anglers fishing from a charter boat where the boat's skipper, with an electronic depth finder locates the shoals of fishes. When located, the anchor is dropped and anglers using handlines or rod and reel can catch these excellent food fishes, literally as fast as the line can be dropped to the bottom. Other popular snappers that make good sport and recreational fishing and fine eating include, among a few other, gray (mangrove snapper), lane snapper, school master, mutton-fish, and dog snapper. All feed on or close to the bottom, often most avidly at night, feeding on all kinds of prey. Except for the red and a few other larger snappers, most frequent both deep and shallow water. The gray or mangrove snapper, a very popular fish among anglers, can be caught in three feet of water or less especially around the mangroves, piers, bridges, and the boat docks. Many of these good tasting small fish can be caught in the surf and other shorelines. Most red snappers weigh about 5 pounds, but 20 pound catches are not uncommon. An occasional fish weighing 30 to 40 pounds is taken, maximum is about 50 pounds.

Methods of fishing vary only slightly from one species to the other. For deep water red snapper a handline or heavy tackle is needed to pull these prize fish from the great depth in which they live, using cut fish (chunks) for bait. None of the other snappers ever weigh more than 2 to 4 pounds. The yellowtail snapper (of Florida) looks quite a bit different than the others. It has a forked tail, color is grayish blue, silvery and pink with a broad yellow stripe that extends from the snout through the eye and along the sides to the tail, above the lateral line. This particular snapper that weighs up to 6 pounds is commonly solitary, often swimming 20 feet or more above the bottom rather than hugging it as the majority of snappers do. The yellowtail is not only a good sport fish but, is equally as good on the table.

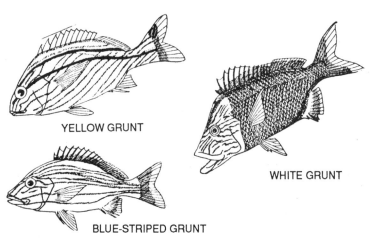

YELLOW GRUNT

WHITE GRUNT

BLUE-STRIPED GRUNT

GRUNTS: There are several hundred species of grunts that are abundant in the warm seas of the world. Their name is derived from the grunting noises they make by grinding their teeth. Most are small and deep bodied fishes. Typically they travel in schools, and all are bottom feeders. In our range the grunts are plentiful in the Atlantic along the shores of the Carolinas and Florida. There are gray grunt, white grunt, yellow grunt, and the pigfish, the latter is north to New York, the others are most abundant around the Florida and Gulf coastlines. The majority of this family of fishes are strictly bottom fishes, and many are very reminiscent to the freshwater sunfishes. Many of them have red mouth parts and most are good eating fish.

PORGY

PORGIES: This family of fish are very similar to the grunts, but in most porgies the body is even more flattened or compressed from side to side. They are medium size to small. Some live offshore while some close inshore. All are often used, whole and alive, for larger game fish bait. However, most are good to eat. The popular northern porgy from the Carolinas to Maine, seldom weigh more than 2 pounds.

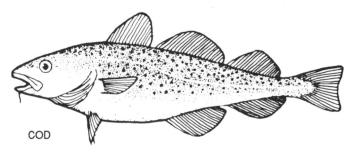

COD

COD: From North Carolina north. A long, deep-bodied fish whose color is somber, browns to grays, with scattered dots; pale below; lateral line white. A chin whisker or barbel is present. This fish inhabits both deep and shallow water, depending on season. Foods includes any marine animal that swims or crawls and will fit into its mouth. Most of the species are harvested commercially. Weight averages 15 pounds, maximum upwards of 250 pounds. Large specimens are often caught in commercial nets. Angler catch usually averages about 7 to 10 pounds for those caught close to shore, and 20 to 25 pounders in offshore water. Natural foods consist of small fishes, molluscs, crabs, seaworms, and other small forms of animal life. Fishing deep, around rocks, by handline or light to medium tackle baited with any of their natural foods will usually prove lucrative.

POLLOCK: This fish is a member of the cod family, and is probably the most popular of the group among anglers. Although found close to shore, on both sides of the Atlantic Ocean, it is commercially netted in depths 400 to 500 feet. It is a greenish in color fish that runs in large schools, most often in deep, cold offshore waters. Deep, slow trolling with fairly heavy equipment using spoons, jigs, etc., spinner baits are also very good especially when used with strip bait. Hook size should be around 9/0. Often times a school of pollock will feed on the surface, the best is trolling slowly around the school then slowly swinging through it, bringing the bait into the school, gets tremendous results. Small pollock are active feeders and are much fun to fish them with saltwater fly rod tackle, using dry and wet flies and streamers. Still

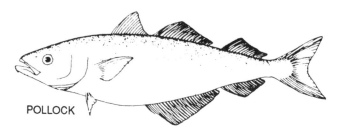

POLLOCK

fishing from a boat or the surf is also enjoyed by many anglers especially in deep bays where crabs are often used as bait. Average weights are from 4 to 10 pounds, but some catches weigh more than 30 pounds.

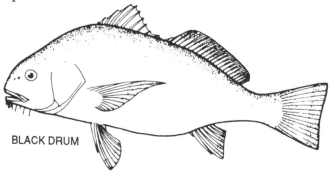

BLACK DRUM

BLACK DRUM: A fish that ranges from Massachusetts to Texas, both in the Atlantic and the Gulf of Mexico. It is a large-scaled, deep-bodied fish with chin whiskers or barbels, body is silvery gray with some, almost indistinct, dark vertical stripes, young are more brilliantly striped while old specimens are entirely without. Large, tough, sharp spines are present in the foreward portion of the dorsal fin. This fish feeds mainly on crabs and molluscs, the shell or shells of the latter are crushed by large throat teeth. In bays, over oyster beds at high tide, fishing and in the surf at high tide. Fiddler and other crabs, clams, and shrimp are the baits. Very rarely ever hit artificials, although jigging with a piece of shrimp will sometimes work. Large drum are fair eating, small specimens are good.

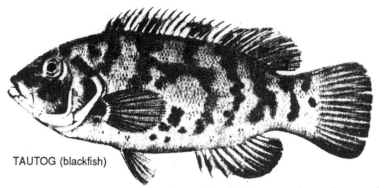

TAUTOG (blackfish)

TAUTOG or BLACKFISH: This fish ranges from the carolinas north. It is a chunky, steep-headed, dark mottled fish of rocky bottoms around bays, coves, and inlets, where they feed on assorted shellfish. Average weight, 2 to 5 pounds, maximum up to 20 pounds. Usually caught by anglers still-fishing from small boats just offshore in about 20 to 30 feet of water or casting in the surf and fishing deep holes along rocky shorelines. Crabs and clams are the most popular natural baits. Hook size should be around a 4/0. A good scraper that makes fine eating. Coloration; Young fish are usually brown or greenish brown with irregular dark mottling or blotchy on the flanks. Large specimens may be entirely black or charcoal gray, often with greenish overtones, or they may be mottled with brown, black, and white. The belly and chin are almost always white or gray, and sometimes with spots on the chin. This fish's availability, year round, combined with its large size and stubborness when hooked makes it a popular sport fish, especially among party boat anglers. Flesh is of fine quality.

SHEEPSHEAD: A popular, fun to catch fish ranges from Cape cod to the Gulf of Mexico. A chunky, deep-bodied fish with large scales and wide black vertical stripes on the body. Dorsal spines are long and very sharp."Buck" teeth which are used for cutting up shellfish and crabs are sheeplike and the reason for this fishes name. It is found around pilings of piers, bridges, and also found around reefs and wrecks. Average weight 1 to 5 pounds; maximum over 20 pounds. Still-fishing with fiddler crab as bait is the popular method of fishing for the sheepshead. Whole or cut shrimp are also good for bait. Wire leader and good sharp hooks are needed. Their

91

SHEEPSHEAD

mouth, although small is extremely hard. It is a wary fish with a soft bite. Some experience is needed before an angler can set the hook on every nibble. Sheepshead are excellent table fish.

FLOUNDERS: Also called fluke, are fishes that occur in the Atlantic Ocean from Maine to South Carolina and on to all of Florida. There are several species, all unmistakable because of their extremely compressed bodies, the fact that both eyes are on one side of the head, and they lie on the bottom, flat on one side. Flounders usually lie buried in the sand or mud, but they can swim swiftly to capture prey or escape from predators. Coloration, depending on the species; upperside dark, mottled, or spotted, underside always white. There are summer flounder, winter flounder, Halibut, California halibut, etc. As a rule flounders run from 1 to 20 pounds, the halibuts much larger, especially the Atlantic species, which weigh up to several hundred pounds. All are fishes of sandy bottoms, in both very shallow and very deep waters. Food consists of all kinds of shellfish, and small fin fish. Methods of fishing is usually still-fishing in bays, etc., from small boats or jetties and piers, using small hooks and keeping bait on the bottom. Baited hook should be frequently moved because flounders are not very active swimmers. They prefer to lie buried in the sand and wait for prey to come by, crawling or swimming. Slow drift fishing, either with live minnows or cut shrimp, or slow trolling with small spinners, is also effective and helps to attract the fish. All flounders are fair fighters and their flesh is delicately delicious.

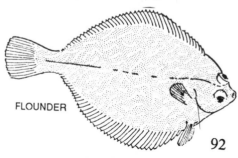
FLOUNDER

92

There are many other saltwater fish which make good catching and fine eating, the huge schools of Silver Hake of the northern Atlantic Coast, the surf-loving whiting, the various rockfish of the Pacific, the California sand and kelp basses, and many others. If, however, you master the exciting art of successful angling for those covered here which best suit your location and opportunities, you will easily be able to catch any of the others you desire. In fact, the chances are that you will probably catch them when you are not even fishing for them!

SHARKS AND SHARK FISHING

AN ANGLER'S GUIDE TO SHARKS

1. Entire body flattened like a skate (one possibility) ANGEL SHARK
2. Large fleshy projection (barbel) present on each nostril, caudal (tail) fin not separated into two lobes (one possibility) NURSE SHARK
3. Anal fins are not present (two possibilities) SPINY DOGFISH KITEFIN SHARK
4. Caudal (tail) fin is long as rest of body (two possibilities)
A. Eye very large BIGEYE THRESHER
B. Eyes small THRESHER SHARK
5. Head is expanded sideways like a shovel or hammer (four possibilities
A. Head shovel-shaped BONNETHEAD SHARK
B. Head Hammer-shaped, anterior margin of head rounded or straight SMOOTH HAMMERHEAD
C. Head Hammer-shaped, anterior margin of head indented, upper and lower teeth serrated or sawlike, posterior margin of pelvic fins curved GREAT HAMMERHEAD

D. Head hammer-shaped, anterior margin of head indented, upper and lower teeth smooth, posterior margin of pelvic fins straight SCALLOPED HAMMERHEAD

6. Mouth at tip of snout and 6 to 7 prominent ridges occur along the entire length of the back (one possibility) WHALE SHARK

7. A mid-dorsal ridge is present between the first and second dorsal fin (six possibilities)

A. First and second dorsal fins are about equal in size SMOOTH DOGFISH

B. Origin of first dorsal fin over or anterior of free inner angle of pectoral fin SANDBAR SHARK

C. Free tip of second dorsal fin is more than twice as long as height of the fin SILKY SHARK

D. Fins tipped in white, length of pectoral fin equal to or greater than distance from mouth to last gill opening WHITETIP SHARK

E. None of the above, upper and lower teeth serrated or sawlike DUSKY SHARK

8. Ridge on caudal peduncle (5 possibilities)

A. Gill openings are as long length of pectoral fins BASKING SHARK

B. Two ridges or lateral keels present on caudal peduncle PORBEAGLE SHARK

C. Uper lobe of caudal (tail) fin is at least three times longer than the lower lobe TIGER SHARK

D. None of the above, upper and lower teeth serrated or sawlike WHITE SHARK

E. None of the above, upper and lower teeth smooth SHORTFIN MAKO SHARK

9. No mid-dorsal keel or ridges on caudal peduncle, both dorsal fins nearly equal in size (two possibilities)

A. All five gill openings in front of pectoral fins SAND TIGER SHARK

B. Head very broad and slightly flattened above. Distance nostril greater than distances from front of mouth to tip of snout BULL SHARK.

IGFA GAME SHARKS

For many years all sharks were considered a menace by all but the shark anglers. However, in recent years, many big game anglers have come to recognize some sharks as a challenging sport fish, and in some species a very high quality food fish. As all anglers who had ever tied into a shark of any size and any species will attest that all sharks will fight for their life when hooked, and that most sharks are capable of long runs, and many are capable of great leaps, spins, powerful head shaking, and even some tail-walking. Experienced shark anglers parallel the tenacity of some sharks with the combined efforts of some *bony fish fighters as tuna, sails, sword, and tarpon. In fact the International Game Fish Association (OGFA) has included seven sharks on their game fish list; the BLUE, MAKO, HAMMERHEAD, PORBEAGLE, THRESHER, TIGER and the GREAT WHITE SHARK of "Jaws" fame. All of these are available to the angler that fishes the South Atlantic Ocean, the Gulf of Mexicao and some are in the Pacific Ocean.

Shark fishing is very much like fishing for any other game fish; to pursue with success any branch of fishing, the senses and habits of fishes to be fished should be carefully studied. When it comes to feeding, sharks, like many other fishes are opportunists, but usually less selective in their choice of food.

*Sharks are without true bone in their skeleton which consist entirely of cartilage, as are the rays and skates.

SHARK IDENTIFICATION

It is very important for all shark anglers to learn the superficial structure or characteristics of sharks. Unlike the bony fishes, sharks only come in three basic colors, brown, gray or blue. Like bony fishes, however, positive identification of sharks began with body outline. Except for a few subspecies all sharks are different in overall design. In fact, many marine biologists, serious scuba divers, and experienced shark anglers are able to identify sharks by silhouette drawings.

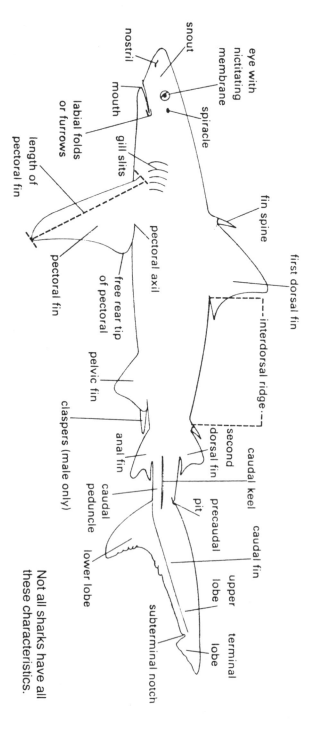

eye with
nictitating
membrane

snout

nostril

mouth

labial folds
or furrows

gill slits

length of
pectoral fin

spiracle

fin spine

first dorsal fin

interdorsal ridge

pectoral axil

free rear tip
of pectoral

pectoral fin

pelvic fin

anal fin

claspers (male only)

second
dorsal fin

caudal keel

precaudal
pit

caudal
peduncle

caudal fin

upper   terminal
lobe   lobe

lower lobe

subterminal notch

Not all sharks have all
these characteristics.

96

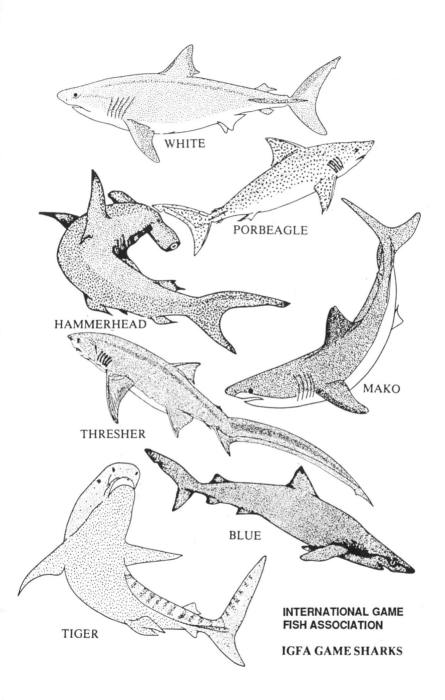

WHITE

PORBEAGLE

HAMMERHEAD

THRESHER

MAKO

BLUE

TIGER

INTERNATIONAL GAME FISH ASSOCIATION

IGFA GAME SHARKS

FISHING TIPS

Have you ever stopped to wonder why some guys seem to always come back with fish? Luck? Not exactly. Steady fishing is a combination of many considerations.

Reels, for instance, are indispensable casting machines that should be oiled, adjusted, and running as smooth as a fine watch before put into use. Too many fishermen completely ignore their reel until it malfunctions. This could happen in the middle of a fight with the biggest fish of your entire lifetime. How about the rod? Guides should be checked for breaks, rough spots and the windings. Ferrules should be tight, shaft free of fractures. The line? Check the first three to six feet for nicks, abrasion and brittleness. Should any of these problems appear, discard the length of the trouble plus an extra foot for insurance. And be sure the knot you tie is one that will hold under tension. The leader - be it monofilament or wire, should get the same inspection as the line. Everything ready? Next is the control of your tackle when fishing from a boat. Spare rods should be secure in proper holders, tackle box closed and secured, loose lures should be hung where someone won't sit on them and above all, enough space allowed between casters so they won't hook each other. As to hooks, make certain the hooks you use are extremely sharp when you buy them. Then keep them that way. In many cases the fish must set the hook when it strikes.

The average fisherman uses a limber rod which makes it virtually impossible to set the hook hard when a fish hits. The light line and drag has the same tendency. You must have the drag fairly light to keep from breaking the line and yet when adjusted in that manner it is almost impossible to really set the hook on the strike.

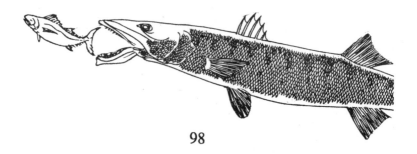

SALTWATER FISH
PREFERRED TEMPERATURE CHART
All readings are in Fahrenheit

Albacore 59 Degrees
Amberjack 60 Degrees
Atlantic Cod 44-49+ Degrees
Atlantic Bonito 64 Degrees
Mackerel 46 Degrees
Barracuda 75 Degrees
Black Marlin 75-70 Degrees
Bluefin Tuna 68 Degrees
Bluefish 68 Degrees
Blue Marlin 78 Degrees
Bonefish 75 Degrees
Dolphin (fish) 75 Degrees
King Mackerel 65 Degrees
Permit 72 Degrees
Pollock 50 Degrees

Pompano 77 Degrees
Red Drum (redfish) 71 Degrees
Red Snapper 57 Degrees
Sailfish 79 Degrees
Sand Seatrout 95 Degrees
Snook 70-75 Degrees
Spotted Seatrout 72 De
Striped Bass 60 Deg.
Yellowtail Calif. 65 Deg.
Swordfish 58 Degrees
Tarpon 76 Degrees
Tautog 70 Degrees
Wahoo 70-86 Degrees
White Marlin 70-80 De.
Winter Flounder 48-52

All fish have a lower and upper tolerance which will average about 10 degrees variance. For instance the striped bass prefers a water temperature of 60 degrees with a lower avoidance temperature of 54 degrees F. which means it will not usually be found in water temperatures ranging below 54 degrees F. while its upper avoidance is 77 degrees F. and will leave the area should the water temperature rise much above 77 degrees F.

The knot you tie can mean the difference between losing or landing a fish. The knots on the following pages have been proven effective in use. If properly formed and if a quality product line is used, they should test close to or equal to the breaking load of the line.

A few basic rules can assure that knots will deliver their full potential in holding power: (1) Where turns are required around the standing line, keep them separated, then pull them together in a neat spiral when tightening the knot; (2) Such knots hold best in low pound class lines. Increased line diameters make it difficult to pull coils tight. Don't expect full rated strength from knots like the Improved Clinch in lines over the 20-lb (10 kg) class; (3) When double lines are used, as in the Palomar or Spider Hitch, keep them as parallel as possible. Avoid twisting as knot is being tied; (4) Always pull knots up as tightly as possible with even, steady pressure. Knot slippage under pressure can cut the line.

Knots to hold terminal tackle

These are vital connections between your line and the terminal tackle. The following knots have proven to be dependable:

IMPROVED CLINCH KNOT
An old standby.

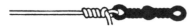

1. Pass line through eye of hook, swivel or lure. Double back and make five turns around the standing line. Hold coils in place; thread end of line through first loop above the eye, then through big loop, as shown.

2. Hold tag end and standing line while coils are pulled up. Take care that coils are in spiral, not lapping over each other. Slide tight against eye. Clip tag end.

The fishing knots on these pages are reprinted courtesy of the Du Pont Company, Wilmington, Delaware from "Fishing Knots You Can Depend On…"

PALOMAR KNOT
Easier to tie right, and consistently the strongest knot known to hold terminal tackle.

1. Double about 4" of line and pass loop through eye.

2. Let hook hang loose and tie overhand knot in doubled line. Avoid twisting the lines and don't tighten knot.

3. Pull loop of line far enough to pass it over hook, swivel or lure. Make sure loop passes completely over this attachment.

4. Pull both tag end and standing line to tighten. Clip about ⅛" from knot.

SPIDER HITCH

This is a faster, easier knot to form a double line.
Under steady pressure it is equally strong but does not
have the resilience of the Bimini Twist under sharp
impact. Not practical with lines above the 30-lb (15
kg) class.

1. Form a loop of the leader length desired. Near the
point where it meets the standling line, twist a section
into a small reverse loop.

2. Hold small loop between thumb and forefinger with
thumb extended well above finger and loop standing
out beyond end of thumb.

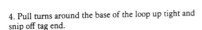

3. Wind double line around both thumb and loop,
taking five turns. Pass remainder of large loop through
the smaller one and pull to make five turns unwind off
the thumb.

4. Pull turns around the base of the loop up tight and
snip off tag end.

Attaching swivel or snap to double line

OFFSHORE SWIVEL KNOT

1. Slip loop end of double line through eye of swivel.
Rotate loop end a half-turn to put a single twist
between loop and swivel eye.

2. Pass the loop with the twist over the swivel. Hold
end of the loop, plus both legs of the double line with
one hand. Let swivel slide to the other end of the
double loops now formed.

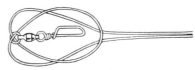

3. Still holding loop and lines with one hand, use
other to rotate swivel through center of both loops, at
least six times.

4. Continue holding both legs of double line tightly
but release end of loop. Pull on swivel and loops of
line will begin to gather.

5. To draw knot tight, grip swivel with pliers and pus
loops toward eye with fingers, while still keeping
standing lines of the double line pulled tight.

The Uni-Knot System

One basic knot which can be varied to meet virtually
every knot-tying need in either fresh or saltwater
fishing. That was the objective of Vic Dunaway,
author of numerous books on fishing. Here is the
system which resulted.

1. TYING TO TERMINAL TACKLE

A. Run line through eye of hook, swivel or lure at
least 6" and fold to make two parallel lines. Bring en
of line back in a circle toward hook or lure.

B. Make six turns with tag end around the double line and through the circle. Hold double line at point where it passes through eye and pull tag end to snug up turns.

C. Now pull standing line to slide knot up against eye.

D. Continue pulling until knot is tight. Trim tag end flush with closest coil of knot. Uni-Knot will not slip.

2. LOOP CONNECTION

Tie same knot as above to point where turns are snugged up around standing line. Slide knot toward eye until loop size desired is reached. Pull tag end with pliers to maximum tightness. This gives lure a natural free movement in water. When fish is hooked, knot will slide tight against eye.

3. JOINING LINES

A. Overlap ends of two lines of about same diameter for about 6". With one end, form Uni-Knot circle, crossing the two lines about midway of overlapped distance.

B. Tie basic Uni-Knot, making six turns around the two lines.

Loop knots

The next two knots, Surgeon's End Loop and Dropper Loop, provide loop connections to attach leaders or other terminal tackle quickly.

SURGEON'S END LOOP

1. Double end of line to form loop and tie overhand knot at base of double line.
2. Leave loop open in knot and bring doubled line through once more.

3. Hold standing line and tag end and pull loop to tighten knot. Size of loop can be determined by pulling loose knot to desired point and holding it while knot is tightened. Clip end ⅛" from knot.

DROPPER LOOP

To form a loop which stands out from line above sinker or other terminal rig.

1. First, form a loop in the line.
2. Pull one side of the loop down and begin taking turns with it around the standing line. Keep point where turns are made open so turns gather equally on each side.

3. After eight to ten turns, reach through center opening and pull remaining loop through. Keep finger in this loop so it will not spring back.

4. Hold loop with teeth and pull both ends of line, making turns gather on either side of loop.

5. Set knot by pulling lines as tightly as possible. Tightening coils will make loop stand out perpendicular to line.

Knots to form double lines

Used primarily for offshore trolling, a double line creates a long loop of line which is stronger than the single strand of the standing line.

BIMINI TWIST

These directions apply to tying double lines of around five feet or less. For longer double-line sections, two people may be required to hold the line and make initial twists.

1. Measure a little more than twice the footage you'll want for the double line. Bring end back to standing line and hold together. Rotate end of loop 20 times, putting twists in it.

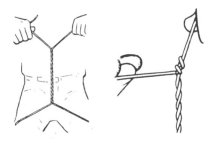

2. Spread loop to force twists together about 10" below tag end. Step both feet through loop and bring it up around knees so pressure can be placed on column of twists by spreading knees apart.

3. With twists forced tightly together, hold standing line in one hand with tension just slightly off the vertical position. With other hand, move tag end to position at right angle to twists. Keeping tension on loop with knees, gradually ease tension of tag end so it will roll over the column of twists, beginning just below the upper twist.

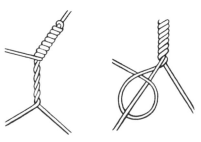

4. Spread legs apart slowly to maintain pressure on loop. Steer tag end into a tight spiral coil as it continues to roll over twisted line.

5. When spiral of tag end has rolled over column of twists, continue keeping knee pressure on loop and move tag end which has held standing line down to grasp knot. Place finger in crotch of line where loop joins knot to prevent slippage of last turn. Take half-hitch with tag end around nearest leg of loop and pull up tight.

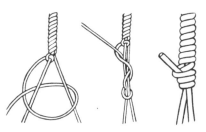

6. With half-hitch holding knot, release knee pressure but keep loop stretched out tight. Using remaining tag end, take half-hitch around both legs of loop, but do not pull tight.

7. Make two more turns with the tag end around both legs of the loop, winding inside the bend of line formed by the loose half-hitch and toward the main knot. Pull tag end slowly, forcing the three loops to gather in a spiral.

8. When loops are pulled up neatly against main knot, tighten to lock knot in place. Trim tag end about ¼" from knot.

JANSIK SPECIAL
A knot of proven strength.

1. Run about five inches of line through eye of hook on lure; bring it around in a circle and run it through again.

2. Make a second circle, parallel with the first, and pass end of line through eye a third time.

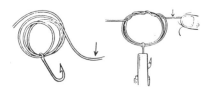

3. Bend standing part of line around the two circles. Bring tag end around in a third circle and wrap it three times around the three parallel lines.

4. Hold hook, swivel or lure with pliers. Hold standing line with other hand and tag end in teeth. Pull all three to tighten. (Arrows identify standing line.)

SNELLING A HOOK.
Using this common snell, hook and leader combinations can be made up to suit the length and strength needed for various types of fishing.

1. Insert one end of leader material through eye of hook just past turn and barb. Pass other end through eye in opposite direction, leaving large loop hanging down.

2. Hold both lines along shank. Use line hanging from eye to wind tight coils around shank and both lines from eye toward hook. Take 5 to 10 turns.

3. Move fingers to hold coils tightly in place. Pull leader extending from eye until entire loop has passed under coils.

4. With coils snugged up neatly, use pliers to pull tag end, cinching up snell. Clip off tag end.

Knots to tie line to line and line to leader

The two knots most often used to join line. The blood knot for two lines of about the same diameter—the surgeon's knot to join a leader to line where the diameters vary considerably.

BLOOD KNOT

1. Lay ends of lines alongside each other, overlapping about 6″ of line. Hold lines at midpoint. Take five turns around standing line with tag end and bring end back between the two strands, where they are being held.

CARING FOR YOUR FISH

The fish you catch should be kept alive in the water from which they have been removed. This is made possible by placing them either on a stringer or in a floating live bag. Some boats are equipped with a live box which manages to protect your fish from the direct rays of the sun. Light, inexpensive Styrofoam ice boxes with ice are very good for keeping your fish fresh.

If you have to keep your fish fresh for a few days before getting them home to the freezer they should be cleaned at the end of each fishing day. When cleaned they should be wrapped in plastic and packed in ice or frozen with dry ice. When using natural ice make sure that the thaw-water does not make direct contact with the fish or it will soak the flesh soft and render it tasteless.

When home and preparing fish for the freezer do so by placing the whole, gutted, with or without scales, headless fish in a half gallon milk carton and then fill it to the top with water and place in freezer, uncovered. When thawed completely, prior to preparing for cooking, the fish can then be scaled, filleted or steaked, whatever your choice. Do not freeze fish fillets in this manner as much of the flavor is lost during the thawing period. Fillets should be wrapped in plastic and then wrapped again in freezer paper. In any case date your packages. Fish can be kept frozen for a period of three months with no changes to the flesh.

FILLETING FISH

The enjoyment that comes from eating fresh fish is greatly enhanced if you don't have to spend a lot of time picking out bones. Especially if you have small children who cannot do the job themselves.

The flavor of most fish is much improved by filleting and I feel it should be done to all species of salt water fishes. The basic requirement is a sharp fillet knife. If you follow the steps as described, you should have no problem.

1. Lay the fish on a cutting board. Make the first cut behind the gill, at a diagonal, cutting toward the head. Stop at the backbone.

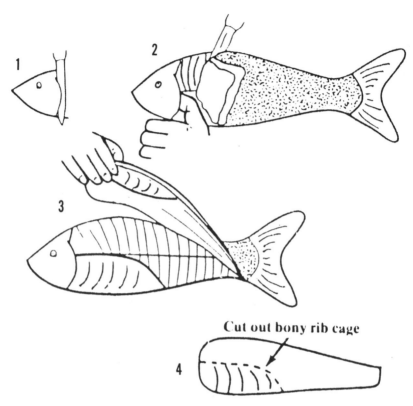

Cut out bony rib cage

2. Turn the blade of the knife, flat against the backbone and cut the length and width off of the body, through the rib cage, and then follow the backbone to the tail fin. Do not cut through skin at the base of the tail. Leave intact and lift the fillet meat off the backbone.

3. Flip the fillet, like opening a hinged lid, and lay it back against the cutting board (still attached by the piece of skin at the tail). Skin the fillet by running the knife between the meat and skin. Now, turn the fish over, and repeat this procedure.

4. The final step is to cut the rib cage out of the fillet meat - result; boneless fillets.

KEEPING YOUR HOOKS SHARP

Make sure that hooks are sharp when you buy them and then keep them that way.

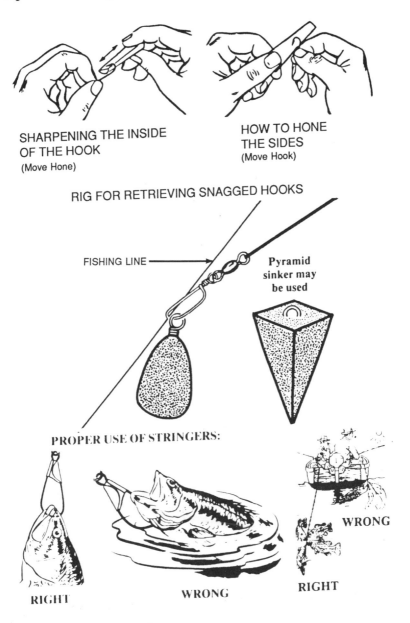

SHARPENING THE INSIDE
OF THE HOOK
(Move Hone)

HOW TO HONE
THE SIDES
(Move Hook)

RIG FOR RETRIEVING SNAGGED HOOKS

FISHING LINE

Pyramid
sinker may
be used

PROPER USE OF STRINGERS:

RIGHT

WRONG

WRONG

RIGHT

107

FIRST AID FOR THE ANGLER

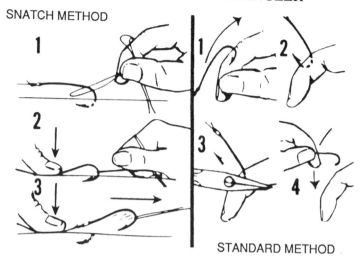

SNATCH METHOD

STANDARD METHOD

METHODS FOR REMOVING FISHHOOKS: Apply antiseptic to hook imbedded area before removal of hook by any of the above illustrated methods are started. After hook is removed allow wound to bleed freely for a couple of minutes before washing it with Betadine and applying an anti-biotic salve. Cover with Band Aid. Should the hook be deeply imbedded into the flesh or is close to, or in the eye, temple, or spine, seek medical help immediately, preferably at an emergency medical center or hospital. In an emergency situation do not attempt to remove the hook by any method.

Necessary items for emergency kit: (1) Gauze pads (2 x 2 inches), (2) Roll of one-inch adhesive tape, (3) Band Aids (a variety of sizes), (4) Un-opened single-edged razor blades, (5) Small pair of wire cutters, (6) Pair of tweezers, (7) Aspirin tablets, (8) Salt Tablets, (9) Alcohol - two ozs. plastic bottle, (10) Betadine - two ozs. plastic bottle, (11) Tube of anti-biotic salve, (12) Alcohol sponges, (13) Pre-sunburn lotion, (14) O'yes - Adolph's Unseason Meat Tenderizer???

Be sure that your tetanus shots are up to date. This precautionary measure alone will prevent many unnecessary infections related to fishing accidents.

FIRST AID TREATMENTS

The following treatments for accidents are suggested because all are proven remedies.

Fish hook removal method

Apply antiseptic before removing the hook. After the hook is removed allow the wound to bleed freely for a couple of minutes before washing it with Betadine and applying the anti-biotic salve. Cover with Band Aid. If the hook is imbedded deep into the flesh or is close to - or in the eye, temple or spine, see a doctor immediately.

Catfish spines

Do not take it lightly. Let wound bleed freely, wash for a few minutes with Betadine and apply anti-biotic salve and cover with a Band Aid.

Stingray wound

Place stricken area in hottest water possible. Keep immersed for 30 minutes to an hour. Pain will be relieved. If wound is large, a physician may be required to close it. When fishing in the surf, boat shoes should be worn, even then, shuffle your feet to scare off the stingrays that may be buried in the sand.

Sea urchin spines

All spines should be removed carefully. If area appears red and painful swelling around the spine punctures occurs, surgery treatment is suggested for the removal of broken spines that might have remained in the flesh. Here again - boat shoes in the surf.

Fish bites

Most fish bites can be treated in the same manner of the catfish sting. However, if the bite is severe like that from a shark or barracuda, apply a tourniquet or direct pressure to stop the bleeding. See a doctor immediately.

Jellyfish and sea anemone stings

Symptoms are blisters, rash, vomiting accompanied by pain in the affected area. Remove tentacles with cloth or paper. Mix paste of alcohol and Unseasoned Adolph's Meat Tenderizer. Cover stings with paste, and then bandage. If the stings cover a wide area and the pain is severe and you have not had a recent tetanus shot, see a doctor as soon as possible. Stay clear of all jelly fishes.

Over heating

Reduce exposure and take one or two salt tablets every two or three hours. Drink adequate fluids. If symptoms are beyond the mild stomach cramp stage, such as dizziness or shock signs, seek immediate care from a doctor.

Sunburn

Lotion or opaque cream like zinc oxide should be made available for over exposure. Fishermen should always wear sufficient clothing and head cover. If burned, but not blistered, apply cold milk compresses every 30 minutes for several hours, then treat with mild lotion like Noxema. Good Polaroid sun glasses are a must.

USE SUNTAN LOTION OR OIL?

If you use any kind of suntan lotion or oil wash your hands well. If no soap is available use sand and salt water. These substances will not only tend to rot your fishing line but could also render your live or artificial baits useless.

GLOVES

Always keep a good pair of work gloves handy to avoid line-burn, or cuts and scratches when removing your catch from the hook. They are also protection from the poisonous spines of the sea cats and the spines and teeth from other fishes, particularly barracuda and bluefish.

DETERMINING THE WEIGHT OF A DEAD FISH
WITH A TAPE MEASURE
(Sharks and bony fishes)

The International Game Fish Association has devised a mathematical formula that enables an angler to obtain the approximate weight of a shark or any other deep bodied fish. The formula is:

$$\frac{Girth\ 2 \times Length}{800} = Weight$$

All this really means is that the girth, or measurement in inches around the fish, is squared (multiplied by itself). This figure is then multiplied by the fishs' length in inches, and the final result is divided by 800. For instance; if a fishs' girth measurement (circumference) at its thickest part is 30 inches, and its length from tip of snout to fork of tail is 46 inches, apply the formula:

$$\frac{30 \times 30 \times 46}{800} \text{ (or) } \frac{41400}{800} = 51.75 \text{ pounds}$$

The next time you catch a large fish and are able to weigh it, try the formula, and then compare, you will be surprised at how well this works.

OCEAN TEMPERATURE

Temperature plays a very important part in the production and well being of all organisms, on the land and in the water. In warmer waters the growth rate of all organisms and the breakdown of dead organic are most rapid. That is, of course, when there is enough nutrients present the productivity of the sea can be extremely high.

Temperature in the open ocean varies from about 28.4 degrees F. to 86 degrees F. Some areas, however, like the Persian Gulf usually exceeds 90 degrees F. during the summer months, and near the shoreline, in shallow water, temperatures as high as 96.8 degrees F. have been recorded. Most of the water in the oceans is much more uniform in temperature; 75 percent is in the range of 32 degrees F. to 42.8 degrees F. and 33% is between 33.8 degrees F. to 42.8 degrees F.

Day by day changes in the temperature of sea water depends upon cloud conditions, but the daily variation is rarely more than 1 degree F., and this change takes place only in a thin surface layer. On a clear day, temperatures may, at times, rise as much as 4 degrees F. The daily change in water temperature is small compared to air or land temperature because about five times as much heat is necessary to produce the same temperature change in water as in air.

In the cold seas water temperature is about equal from the surface to the bottom all year 'round. In the temperate areas a fairly thin layer of the upper surface (only some tens of meters in some places) is warmed up during the summer. In the subtropical and still more in the tropical areas the surface layers become much warmer than the deep and may penetrate down to 600 to 1,500 feet.

The deep and bottom layers of the open oceans are always cold and most of the water comes originally from the Arctic or Antarctic seas. Animal life in these cold-water layers consists of cold-resistant forms which is generally very sparse.